Wild Rice Cooking

Other Books by Susan Carol Hauser

Natural History

Sugartime: The Hidden Pleasures of Making Maple Syrup
Nature's Revenge: The Secrets of Poison Ivy, Poison Oak, and Poison Sumac, and Their Remedies

Nonfiction

Full Moon: Reflections on Turning Fifty
Girl to Woman: A Gathering of Images
Which Way to Look
Meant to Be Read Out Loud
What the Animals Know

Poetry

Redpoll on a Broken Branch

Wild Rice Cooking

Harvesting, History, Natural History, and Lore with 80 Recipes

Susan Carol Hauser

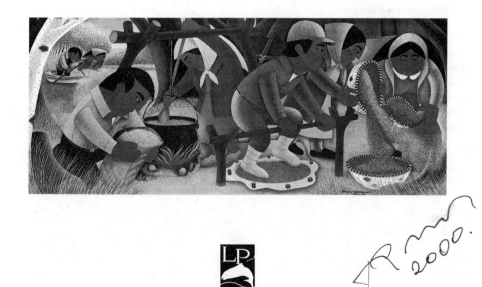

The Lyons Press

Printed in the United States of America

Design by A Good Thing, Inc.
Photographs by Susan Carol Hauser, unless otherwise noted
10 9 8 7 6 5 4 3 2 1

PERMISSIONS
Grateful acknowledgement is made to the following for permission to reprint material:
For photographs and images:
The Minnesota Historical Society, Vivienne Morgan, Greg Kearns, Michael Haramis
For captions, charts, and graphs:
Thomas Vennum, E.A. Oelke, Greg Britton, Paul Addis, R.A. Porter, Alan Grombacher, University of Minnesota Agriculture Extension Service, The University of Minnesota Press, *Cereal Foods World*
For recipes, charts, and graphs:
Minnesota Cultivated Wild Rice Council, Gourmet Harvest
Photographs on chapter opening pages xiv, xxvi, 17, 40, 68 by Vivienne Morgan.
Photograph on chapter opening page 110 by the author.

The Library of Congress Cataloging-in-Publication Data is available on file.

This book is for Bill, my ricing partner, in and out of the canoe.

My thanks to

Vivienne Morgan, for her fine artwork and her patience with writers;
Dave Carlson, for the wild rice canoe trip on the Turtle River;
Carol Jessen-Klixbull, for her fascination with wild rice;
Earl Nyholm, for his insight;
Brian Donovan, for his love of language;
Tom Vennum, for his book *Wild Rice and the Ojibway People*;
E. A. Oelke, for his precision and generosity;
the wild rice experts who told me their stories;
my family and friends who shared their recipes.

Contents

The passionate history and probable future of The Good Berry.

Tables

Prologue: Wild Rice, Ricer, Ricing

North of Bemidji, Minnesota, on Beltrami County Highway Nine, if you follow the road far enough, you will come to a low spot in the terrain. First there is a pasture that slopes toward the road and yields to a large pond, then there is a watercourse.

The watercourse crosses under the highway. In the spring, it is brisk with snowmelt. At its bottom, even then, seeds from last year's *Zizania palustris* are breaking through the muck of the soaked earth. As the water slows to its summer pace, the plants take hold and grow themselves to the surface of the stream.

In June, narrow, delicate leaves unfurl on the water's surface, where they float with the current. In July, the plants' slender stalks, with encouragement from the long sun, breach the water, stretch into air, stand straight, and begin to set flowers.

Around the shore of the pond, and reaching back and out from the stream, more wild rice rises up in its annual ritual of perpetuation. This one stand spreads out for acres to the east and west for as far as a traveler in a car can see.

Every year in late summer when I drive down County Nine, I say to myself, *Maybe I will rice this year.* In northern Minnesota, rice is a verb as well as a noun: "We are going ricing." "I riced last weekend." We say it the way we say "We're going to sugar next week," and everyone knows we mean that we will tap maple trees, harvest the sap, and boil it down to maple syrup.

When I think about going ricing, I know what it means because I have riced. My husband, Bill, had been a ricer for several years. I envied him his time on the river, time in the late summer light, time in the canoe with the water lapping at its sides, time breathing in the primeval aroma of the perimeter swamps. When he came home late in the afternoon, he was wet with sweat and with water from the river. Rice beards, one-inch-long wisps with barbed awns, clung to his clothing. His face was red from the sun and from the effort of his body. He ate dinner like a logger, slept like a bear in winter.

Bill riced with the friends who taught him to rice. One summer, many years ago, I decided it was time for me to experience the human ritual for myself, and as we only needed two people and one canoe, one early September day we hefted the canoe onto the top of the car, tied on the poling pole, put the knockers in the back, along with a lunch and water to drink, and headed out to Pine Point on the Mississippi River, about a twenty-mile drive from home.

Pine Point is a popular setting-off spot for ricers. From it you can paddle against the current and toward Lake Itasca, the cultural headwaters of the Mississippi River, which is about fifteen road miles from Pine Point, and about a day's worth of miles by canoe. Or, you can paddle with the current and away from Lake Itasca.

If you go toward Lake Itasca, you will be traveling south, for from Lake Itasca, the Mississippi River flows north. Near Bemidji, thirty road miles later, it turns east, and seventy-five road miles after that, near Grand Rapids, it finally swings south in its meandering journey to the Gulf of Mexico. The main channel of the river itself is about twelve feet wide, but it only occasionally touches shore, as it does at Pine Point. The rest of the time, it is a narrow ribbon lacing through a half-mile to one-mile-wide swamp underlaced with rivulets and lazy watercourses.

South of Pine Point, toward Itasca, rice lines the river channel in long beds that vary from a few feet to maybe one hundred feet wide. These beds are among the first to get riced out, as they are close to the landing, and because the river water flows easily through them and the canoe does not get bogged down as it does in the shallower beds that reach farther back from the river proper.

But the real ricers, the ones who want a winter's supply of rice, or who plan to sell their harvest, paddle north out of Pine Point. The current helps carry their canoes along, but that is not why they go that way. They are heading to Rice Lake and other backwaters of the main stream of the Mississippi

River. Acres of *Zizania palustris* grow in these natural paddies. For centuries and probably for millennia this wild rice has fed blackbirds and ducks and human beings.

The day my husband took me ricing, we arrived at the Pine Point landing close to mid-morning. It is of no use to go out earlier, because rice that is still damp from the morning dew will not readily release its kernels.

There were already a half dozen cars and pickups there. The ricing teams were down-loading their canoes, and arranging in them their poles and knockers, and cushions and food. We, too, prepared ourselves for our morning's task.

Working at a quiet pace, and talking amiably to each other, the teams of ricers one at a time pulled their canoes over to the landing proper, slid them down the ten-foot-steep embankment into the water, slipped them into the current, and hopped in. As we fussed our way through our preparations, we watched them disappear around the first crook in the river and into the five- to six-foot-tall grasses and reeds that rise from its marshy sides. Although we could no longer see them, we could still hear them talking and laughing as they wended their way with the current toward Rice Lake.

Finally ready, we dragged our canoe over to the bank, pushed it down the steep slope and into the water, and hopped aboard. I was in the stern, where the poler stands. As the current caught us, I started to paddle with it, but Bill said we should go the other way. As this was my first time out, we would go south from the landing, toward Lake Itasca, and away from the "serious" ricers. I did not care which way we went. It was ricing time, and I was on the river, in a canoe, taking in the early September sun and the sounds and smells of the water.

As quickly as the other ricers disappeared from our sight when we stood on the bank, the landing disappeared from our sight as we moved around the first bend in the river, and into a ten-foot-wide tunnel of grasses and reeds that lifted well above our shoulders and had for a roof the glittering September sky.

We paddled a mere fifteen minutes from the landing. Along the way, we passed strips of rice that had been harvested. We could see the paths where the canoes slid into the beds, pressing the rice stalks down and to the sides. As we continued on, Bill watched both sides of the river for a channel that might lead us into an untapped bed.

Finally we found one, an opening in the tall grasses that wafted above our heads. We paddled into it. No one had been there before us, and the rice went back about ten feet on each side of a slender path of open water.

We put our paddles in the canoe, and readied ourselves for the harvest. Bill carefully moved from the front seat of the canoe to the middle, where he knelt facing forward with a lifesaver cushion under each knee. I stood just in front of my seat with one foot lodged against it and to one side, the other forward a bit and to the other side.

There is really no way to practice ricing. You just have to get in a canoe and do it. You do, however, have a choice between two tasks: poling or knocking. By tradition, and now by law, ricers can only pole their canoes through the rice beds. Paddles do not work, because the stands are thick, and because they damage the rice; motors move the canoe too quickly for the action of the knocker, and are considered to be not sporting.

Knockers are also regulated, although anyone who wants to harvest rice efficiently and effectively would want to comply with the traditional standards.

Knockers are sticks that cannot be more than thirty inches long, and cannot weigh more than one pound. To meet these specifications, they have to be made of poplar or a similar lightweight wood. In some families, knockers are passed down from generation to generation.

Bill made the knockers we used. I liked the feel of them in my hand, heavier at the handle, lighter at the tip, the strokes of the carving knife still visible, and the grain of the wood stained with the oil from his hands and from the rice plants. But I did not use the knockers. We decided I should pole. I am shorter than Bill, with better balance.

I had handled the pole before we came out and liked the feel of it as much as of the knockers. It was made from a two-inch-diameter tamarack sapling that was stripped of its branches and bark, but not of the nubs where the branches came out of the trunk. A metal duck bill was attached to the wider end of the pole. It looks a bit like two hands pressed together at their base. A hinge between the two sides allows the "hands" to open. When the pole is pushed into the mud at the bottom of the water, the hands open flat, allowing the poler to purchase the pole against the mercurial muck that serves as ground in these boggy waters.

I grew up playing on Minnesota lakes, and learned early to not stand up in a boat. Standing in the narrow canoe, I understood why in a new way. The slightest shift of my hips caused our slender craft to wobble, and my effort to correct the wobble only made us wobble even more in the other direction.

Fortunately, ricing is leisurely in pace, and while I maneuvered to head the canoe into the rice stand, Bill started his work. He reached out with the knocker in his right hand into the rice that was snugging up against our craft, and sort of encircled the rice with his stick and pulled it over the boat. At almost the same time, he brought his left-hand knocker over to and above the other one, and before the canoe moved forward, and before the rice stalks slipped away from the right-hand knocker, he gently grazed the right knocker with the left, drawing the left one from near the hand on the right one down to its tip.

Instantly I heard the tinkling of rice kernels against the metal bottom of the canoe. As we worked, that sound was lost, because the rice covered the bottom of the canoe, and then filled it, covering Bill's kneeling cushions, and then his knees, and rising up his legs. Then the only sounds were the swooshing of the canoe against the rice stalks, the random clicking of the knockers against each other, and the occasional burst of song from a redwing blackbird rousted by us from its own garnering of the rice.

When I first stood up to take my poling position, I was surprised to realize that I could now see over the stands of flora that so completely encompassed the canoe, could see to the far sides of the river valley, to the banks and trees that keep the water in its place. Scanning the swamp itself, and looking down river, I could even see the tops of the poles and the heads of other ricers, slipping in and out of sight through the high rice as though through shadows.

But I was not there to indulge in the vista, and I turned to my job. Rather quickly, I thought, I gained control of the pole. I nudged the front of the canoe just two feet into the bed, and then worked the pole so that the canoe remained parallel to the watercourse. This way we could go back and forth in a pattern, turning at the end of the bed, and returning just a foot or two over from our previous row. It is the traditional way. The path left by the canoe with each pass can be used again, for wild rice seeds ripen over a period of ten to fourteen days and any given bed can be harvested several times. Neat rows established on the first pass can be reused without breaking down any more rice.

Pleased with myself, and enjoying the sounds and smells around me, I learned something else quickly: it is best to pay attention to your chore. When we finished working the one side of the channel, I turned the canoe to pole across the several feet of open water to get to the other side. I don't remember what I was attending to, but it was not my pole. I had pulled its fifteen-foot-length out of the water, working downward, hand over hand, as I had been doing, and then brought it forward and pushed it back into the water. When the duck bill found bottom and took hold, I worked hand over hand back up the pole, pushing the canoe along until I ran out of wood. Then I pulled the pole again out of the water and repeated the process.

Except this time, when I worked hand over hand up the pole and did not stop when I got to its end. Neither did the canoe, and we glided easily on, my empty hands grasping at the empty air. When I looked back, the pole, now ten feet behind us, was already giving way to gravity, the water working as though hand over hand to pull it under the surface.

The pole floated, of course. Sort of. The duck bill was stuck in the muck, and held that end down. I retrieved my paddle from under the heaps of rice and paddled back to the pole. It was only my pride that was damaged, as it was several times more when I was wooed away from my task by some passing beauty, a duck or an eagle, or even a cloud. But I came to not mind it. When paddling, I could sit down and rest my weary legs, and Bill could rest his weary arms.

We stopped other times, too, to rest and to eat. Then Bill would turn and face me and we'd pass food and drinking water back and forth, and we'd turn our faces to the sky, and our ears to the wind. If we listened carefully, and the breeze was right, we could hear other ricers, their conversation, and the clicking of their sticks muffled by the fabric of the very rice we were gathering.

We did not stay out the day on the water. There was room for more rice in the canoe when our bones and muscles forced us to stop. As the sun started its decline toward the west, we stowed the pole and the knockers, Bill moved up to the front seat from his kneeling position in the middle of the canoe, we reclaimed our paddles from under the rice, and turned back toward the main channel of the river.

One advantage of going upstream to start with is that you get to flow with the current on the return trip. We barely paddled at all, letting the slow water slowly return us to Pine Point. When we got there, other ricers were also returning, some with their canoes filled to the gunwales with seeds of *Zizania palustris*. Unhurriedly, we beached our canoes in the order that we arrived, and dragged them up the bank to the cars and pickups.

Too weary now to talk, most of us worked in silence. Bill and I put the equipment and food packs into the trunk of the car, and I brought a gunnysack back to the canoe. We took turns holding it open while the other scooped rice into it. The awned beards stuck to our clothes, got in our hair, and even down our necks, but we kept scooping. When the bulk of the rice was in, we used our hands to sweep the remainder into little piles, and also scooped that into the sack.

We put the rice in the trunk, then went back for the canoe. As we turned it upside down, a younger, stronger ricing team came over and offered to put it on top of the car for us, and we let them. Then we cinched it down with ropes, climbed into the car, and headed for home. At first we talked a bit, conjecturing about the amount of rice we would have after the raw rice in our gunnysack was processed, but then we did not talk at all, Bill conserving his energy for driving, me for cataloging the effort and pleasure of the day.

That night I ate like a logger and slept like a bear. And I never again asked to go ricing. I think the enormity of the task overcame me, and not just in its physical aspects. I became fatigued, too, by the weight of the overall rite, with its intense cultural history, and I came to feel that I did not belong in the rice beds.

Perhaps my feeling was premonitory, for about that time the raising of wild rice in cultivated paddies harvested by machine became successful, not only in Minnesota, but in California. With abundant and predictable commercial crops, the cost per pound of wild rice plummeted, and harvesting in lakes and rivers declined proportionately. The annual labor-intensive harvest that once provided a pantry staple and seasonal income to families and communities now was worth less than half its dollar value just a few years before.

Ironically, perhaps, the robust cultivated wild rice economy may have saved the natural paddies in lakes and rivers. When the prices were high, many natural paddies were overharvested and not enough rice was allowed to fall into the water to provide for the next year's crop. Rice stands dwindled. Now, with the reduced value of the crop, mostly only those dedicated to the tradition of wild rice return to the ancient beds.

Once again, mostly those who are fed by the rice spiritually as well as physically are the ones who reach into the tall stalks and sweep the rice off the heads and into their laps. Once again, mostly those who understand the needs of the rice are the ones who carefully lace their canoes through the fabric of the rice beds. Once again, the rice is harvested mostly by those who know that one crop seeds the next, and who are pleased when they see precious kernels escape the knockers, find the busy water, and sail away.

When I drive by the County Nine rice beds and conjecture once again about going out to rice, I know I will not do it. I am fed more wholly when I watch the rice grow and fill this watercourse, and then bend from the weight of its own fruit, and then stand erect again after its burden is shaken loose by the wind and by blackbirds that land on the backs of the bent stalks, eating some of the seed and shaking the rest into the water, where some will be eaten by ducks, and some will sink down into the muck and will wait out the winter until it is time to rise again.

The stalks themselves will also fall in time, will enter the water. My life is less simple, but is made simpler by that rhyme.

Manoominike-giizis: Wild Rice Moon

From the prehistoric times of about one thousand years ago to the historic times of approximately four hundred years ago, the Woodland Cultures (Laurel People) of the western Great Lakes area of North America were settled on the shores of the lakes and rivers of land that includes what is now known as northern Minnesota. These peoples were processing wild rice, and developing pottery and burial mound technology. During the same period, the prehistoric peoples to the south, now called the Mississippian Cultures, strongly influenced by Mexican agriculture, were developing agricultural technologies.[1]

During the last of the prehistoric period, the agricultural tradition made its way into what is now southern Minnesota, but the geographical exigencies

1

of the western Great Lakes area did not favor its development farther north. The harvesting and processing of wild rice, along with hunting and fishing, persisted from prehistoric into historic times.[2] Still, there remained a cross-fertilization of influences. Wild rice harvesting continued into the nineteenth century as far south as Nebraska and as far southeast as Illinois.[3] Southern pottery influences are evident in the western Great Lakes area.[4]

"Historic times" are marked in North America by the arrival of the Europeans, who kept written records, often in the form of diaries and reports. These Europeans arrived in the western Great Lakes area in the seventeenth century.[5] The Minnesota area was then populated primarily by the Dakota tribe of the Sioux nation, and the Wisconsin area primarily by the Menominee tribe, meaning "wild rice people," of the Algonquin nation. Both nations harvested wild rice.

The arrival of the Europeans marked the beginning of a westward movement of the eastern populations of what would become the United States. As explorers and fur traders sought new territory, so did the Algonquin Ojibwe people. Originally from the Atlantic coast, they were forced to move west as their lands were appropriated by European settlers.

The transition from Dakota to Ojibwe predominance in Minnesota took nearly two hundred years. The period was marked by increasing strife and warfare between the two tribes, until 1851 when the Dakota were finally forced from the area. However, for a long time the Dakota continued to risk attack by returning to harvest rice in their old territory.[6]

The conflict between the two tribes was in great part over hunting lands that were also wild rice territory.[7] With the incursion of the Europeans, wild rice had become a useful trade commodity in addition to its continuing use as a food staple. Later, it would even "come to be regarded as a luxury by white people," according to a news item in a 1913 issue of the *Scientific American.*

The earliest written descriptions of wild rice confirm its value to any human living or traveling in the area. References to it are found in the 1633 memoir of Pierre Gaultier de Varennes, sieur de la Verendrie;[8] the 1673 writings of Father Jacques Marquette;[9] and in a 1751 scientific tract by Peter Kalm.[10] Perhaps the most eloquent entry comes to us from Pierre d'Esprit sieur Radisson in 1668, in a missive to Charles II of England:

> Our songs being finished we began our teeth to worke. We had there a kinde of rice, much like oats. It growes in the watter in 3 or 4 foote deepe. There is a God that shews himselfe in every countrey, almighty, full of goodnesse and y preservation of those poore people who knoweth him not. They have a particular way to gather up that graine. Two takes a boat and two sticks, by w[ch] they gett y[e] eare downe and gett the corne out of it. Their boat being full, they bring it to a fitt place to dry it; and that is their food for the most part of the winter, and doe dresse it thus: ffor each man a handfull of that they putt in the pott, that swells so much that it can suffice a man.[11]

Knowledge of wild rice harvesting traditions comes to us today primarily from the Ojibwe. Until 1988, with the publication of *Wild Rice and the Ojibwe People,* a definitive work by Thomas Vennum, most of the stories came to us through the observations of non-Indians. Vennum, while drawing from previously published reports, also went to the Indian people and recorded their stories directly.

While there are some differences in detail between the stories recorded by non-Indian observers and those told to Vennum, and even among the stories told to Vennum, there is general agreement regarding the traditional methods of harvesting and processing wild rice.

Manoominike-giizis, the wild rice moon, or the month of making wild rice, usually occurs in late August or early September. In the old times, when the rice set seed and developed toward maturity, the ricing chief of an Ojibwe village would go out frequently to check on its status. No harvesting of the rice would be done until this chief officially opened the season.[12]

Before the rice fully matured, however, the women of the community would usually go out into the rice fields and mark the stands that were theirs. They did this by gathering in a number of stems and binding them together using string made from bark. Each woman tied her bundles in a unique way, thus identifying her stand from others.[13]

The binding of the rice had other benefits as well. It kept the stalks secure and made them less vulnerable to wind, which could knock off ripened seeds, and to birds, which also knocked off seeds when they landed on the stalks to eat from them. And binding made harvesting easier and more efficient.

The binding of the rice was perhaps the first aspect of traditional harvesting to be lost to the changing ways of the middle to late nineteenth century. The Ojibwe speaking to Vennum attribute the decline and cessation of binding to the "breakdown of tradition, premature harvesting, and the incursion of whites."[14] As wild rice became a commodity for sale and trade, competition for the rice beds increased. At the same time, the social restrictions of the Ojibwe villages were in decline. Ricers began going out before the rice was ready for harvest, and the role of the ricing chiefs became diminished.

Until the late 1800s, Ojibwe harvesters tied wild rice prior to harvesting time. Each family had a unique way of tying, or binding, the rice, thus identifying their family's allotment as determined by the village's rice chief. Tying also protected the rice from wind and birds. "Wild rice ready for harvest, Onamia Lake, Minnesota, ca. 1909." Minnesota Historical Society. Reproduced with permission.

The problems with ricers who did not fully respect the crops escalated into the first half of the twentieth century, and reached its apex when harvesters, especially non-Indians, started harvesting rice mechanically. Ralph K. Andrist describes the situation in a July 1951 *Reader's Digest* article: "It took the white man a while to discover that wild rice might be worth exploiting. When he did, motorboats chugged through the rice beds with the effect of an elephant in a field of corn. A mechanical harvester, devised to get more grain in a hurry, ruined many rich beds and the crop was facing destruction."

In 1939, the State of Minnesota passed a Wild Rice Act. It restricted harvesting to traditional methods, requiring that a license be purchased, and that harvesting be done from a canoe propelled by a pole, and that ricers use knockers (flails) to release the rice from the plants. The act also sought to restore order to the ricing process by establishing local ricing committees that would designate the opening of rice fields, a recognition of the vital function of the ricing chief.[15] Today, more than sixty years later, these same restrictions generally apply, except that the opening of the rice fields is determined by the Minnesota Department of Natural Resources (DNR) on non-reservation waters, and by tribal officials on reservation waters.

Although the binding of the rice is known today, even to the Ojibwe, only through stories, most other elements of the traditional ricing harvest have remained in tact. Around the turn of the last century, Indian families still gathered at their traditional ricing camps to knock and process rice. They would have come there from their summer camps where they had gardens, and would go from there to their winter camps, where they continued hunting and fishing. From the winter camps they moved to their sugaring camps, where they made maple syrup, and then on again to the summer camps.[16]

The wild rice camp originally was operated mostly by women. The men could not participate, as they were off on their fall hunt. As the Ojibwe became more involved in the European-style economy taking hold in Minnesota, and as wild rice became a valuable cash crop, the men joined the women in the fall harvest.

The first task of the harvest, after the binding of the rice, was the gathering of the grain. For this the canoe was the perfect vessel. When pushed with a long pole, it slid with relative ease through the tall, thick grasses, where paddles were of little or no use. The poler stood at one end of the canoe; the knocker sat in front of or behind the poler.

The poler pushed the canoe along, and the knocker reached into the rice with one stick and pulled some rice over the canoe. The other stick was used to gently strike the heads of the rice, knocking the ripe kernels into the canoe. A gentle stroke was necessary, as wild rice "shatters," i.e., the kernels on a given head do not all ripen at the same time.

Although the shattering nature of rice is a primary problem today for commercial harvesting of wild rice in cultivated paddies, it was not a problem for

"Grace Rogers and Joe Aitken harvesting wild rice near Walker, Minnesota. 1939. Photo: Monroe Kelly." Minnesota Historical Society. Reproduced with permission.

traditional harvesters. The team simply returned to the stands two or three more times over the course of ten to fourteen days, until the subsequently matured rice was captured. To insure easier and more effective passage through the rice on later passes, the poler was careful to direct the canoe through the stand in a row-by-row pattern. This way, on return trips, the canoe glided more easily through the previously made channels.

Although a rice bed was harvested several times, not all of the kernels ended up in the canoes. Many fell into the water, and served as seed for the next year's crop, and some was just not harvested. It was estimated in 1969 that only five to twenty-five percent of available rice was gathered.[17] Estimates today indicate that now forty to sixty percent of rice is harvested.[18]

The rice that falls into the canoe is encased in a hull that has a barbed awn at one end. As every ricer knows, this awn not only helps pull the rice seed down into the muck on the bottom of the lake or river, but allows it to stick to a ricer's hair and clothes, and even, somehow, to migrate under clothing where it pokes and itches and irritates, reminding the ricer of long ago and of today that this is a wild crop.

The volume of rice taken in by a team of harvesters on a given day is estimated to be between one hundred and three hundred pounds raw (green), equivalent to about forty to one hundred and twenty pounds finished, a ratio of two and a half pounds to one.

The volume of rice taken is affected, as are all crops, by the vagaries of that particular year, and the overall annual take varies considerably. Over a four-year period "a stand can be expected to produce one bumper crop, two fair crops and one failure."[19] Crop failure can be affected by four conditions: high

When the canoe is full of wild rice, harvesters return to the landing. In the early days, Ojibwe families processed the rice at a camp set up near the rice fields. Later, rice was bagged and taken to a commercial processor or sold to rice dealers. "Indians collecting wild rice. Ca. 1920." Minnesota Historical Society. Reproduced with permission.

water levels and fluctuation in water levels; alteration of environmental conditions by a bumper crop; poor pollination (due to weather factors); and insect pests and diseases.[20]

Getting the rice into the canoe is only the first step of getting wild rice to the table. Processing raw rice involves four major steps: drying (curing), parching (scorching), hulling (jigging), and winnowing. These steps are followed not only in the traditional ricing camp but in the processing of cultivated paddy rice.

In the traditional ricing camp, processing almost always took place at the ricing site. As late as 1924, such camps were still being used in northern Minnesota, as Donald Hough describes in "Ancient Harvest in Our Own Northwest" (to an easterner in 1924, the Midwest was still the west). "More than one visitor to the Minnesota woods has wondered at the strange skeletons, made of saplings, which gleam in the sunlight on the shores of so many lakes. They stand there all summer long; shiny weather-beaten poles and bark withes. . . . They are usually in groups; two or three here, three or four there. They vary in shape from the conical wigwam to a rounded mound. . . ."

But in the autumn, says Hough, the frames overnight "have mysteriously grown a skin of shining birchbark. . . . Smoke comes from the openings at the tops . . . and yellow bark canoes appear on the sand beaches. . . ."

In 1924, by the end of the first day of ricing, processing equipment will also have appeared: tarps for curing the rice, an iron kettle for parching, and birch bark baskets for winnowing. In the old times, skins or woven mats were used instead of tarps, and drying racks instead of iron kettles that came west to Minnesota with the Ojibwe. But the work remained the same.

When the rice was brought in from the lake or river, it was in a vulnerable state.[21] If it was not dried within a few days, it would become moldy, and would be useless. However, if it was kept wet it would not be vulnerable to mold. Thus, rice that was not immediately dried was usually kept wetted with water until it could be properly spread out.

For the drying process, the rice was spread about six to twelve inches deep on tarps in the sun. It usually was dried for a day so that some moisture could escape from the kernels, and rice that was not fully ripened could be finished.

The rice was turned frequently during the drying period, and was picked over to remove leaves and other detritus.

When the rice was sufficiently dried, it was parched. Parching "serves two main purposes: destroying the germ prevents the kernel from sprouting so that it can be kept indefinitely; hardening the kernel loosens the tight-fitting hull so it can be broken off and discarded."[22]

Hand-processed wild rice was parched in cast-iron kettles or in metal washtubs. Prior to these conveniences, the rice was parched in a variety of

In the early days, rice was parched by hand at the ricing camp. "Grace Rogers parching wild rice. Leech Lake, 1939." Photo: Monroe Killy. Minnesota Historical Society. Reproduced with permission.

ways. Usually it was dried and smoked on racks. Sometimes it was parched on hot stones, or in clay pits.[23]

In any situation, parching usually took about fifteen minutes to an hour. A small amount of rice was placed in the kettle, which was set at an angle over a fire. The rice was stirred continually with a paddle until it was done. Doneness was determined by breaking open a kernel. It would have gone from soft white to crystalline white.

Once the rice was parched, it was ready to be hulled. Hulling was perhaps the most difficult part of traditional processing. Enough pressure had to be applied to the kernels so that the now crisp hulls broke away, but not so much pressure that the kernels themselves broke. This delicate balance was accomplished by "jigging" the rice. A container the size of a large bucket was fitted into a hole in the ground. Parched rice was placed in the bucket, and then was treaded by a person wearing special moccasins who leaned on two poles placed at angles over the jig pit.[24] When the hulls were loosened and had fallen off the kernel, the hulling was done.

There were many variations of the jig pit, including a clay pit discovered in Michigan that dates back to the prehistoric Woodland period.[25] Other variations included pits lined with skins, wood slat pits and, more recently, washtub pits. Occasionally, rice was hulled using pestles.[26]

When the rice had been jigged, the hardest of the work was done. Winnowing, the next and final stage, removed the dust and broken hulls from the rice. For this, the rice was placed in a shallow basket or tray and was tossed up gently into the air in a breeze. The chaff blew away, and the rice was finished.

Finished rice was stored in many ways, including in grass or birch bark baskets, or in skin baskets or sacks.[27] Later, gunnysacks were used, and now a woven plastic sack is popular.

In the early days, parched wild rice was placed in a "jig pit" for threshing and danced on with new moccasins. This separated the rice from its hull. "Wild rice harvesting, ca. 1938." Minnesota Historical Society. Reproduced with permission.

At the traditional Ojibwe ricing camp, the first finished rice was cooked and served at a ceremonial feast of thanksgiving, which paid homage to the spirits that gave wild rice to the people. Maude Kegg describes such a feast in *Portage Lake: Memories of an Ojibwe Childhood*: "When she finished the rice, no one was supposed to eat any, so I was forbidden to eat any. First she gave a feast in which she offered tobacco and talked about the manitous and thunderbirds, and the sun, and all such things, and put tobacco out. When she finished speaking, we ate the rice."[28]

Even among hand-harvesters, it is rare today for wild rice to be hand-processed. Rather it is sold for cash outright to large processors, or is taken to smaller, local processors where it may also be sold outright for cash. Ricers who want to keep their rice for personal use take it to small operations for processing, as my husband and I did. Hand-processed rice is rarely sold, but rather is kept and used within the community.

Small processors carry out three of the four major steps of wild rice processing using mechanized equipment. The rice is still dried on tarps, but it is parched by turning it in large, metal barrels heated by a wood fire or sometimes by propane gas. It is then hulled and winnowed by machine.

Although scientists tell us that all wild rice used for food is the same species, *Zizania palustris,* our larger selves tell us something else. It is commonly

After the rice was parched and hulled, it was winnowed, to remove the rice from the chaff. "Ojibwe woman fanning wild rice. 1937." Minnesota Historical Society. Reproduced with permission.

believed, especially in wild rice country, that wild rice gathered from lakes and rivers and processed by hand or at small operations offers us something in addition to innate good taste. It offers the mysteries of *manoomin,* and the blessings of the harvest carried out under *manoominike-giizis,* the moon of the making of wild rice.

The Good Berry

W e love wild rice in our house. When I make it, I cook a whole one-pound bag and freeze the leftovers in one-cup packages. When I come home tired from work, and am hungry in body and spirit, I put a package in the microwave to thaw, and then stir into it a can of black beans, add a little cumin for seasoning, heat it up, and in ten minutes I have a meal that satisfies both of my hungers.

It is likely that wild rice enriched the dinner table of prehistoric peoples living in the western Great Lakes area, and its rich nutritional content made it a staple in the diet of American Indians. Its durability after processing made it even more valuable, for unlike many seasonal foods, it could be successfully

Table I NUTRITIONAL COMPARISON	Wild Rice	Long-Grain Brown Rice	Parboiled Long-Grain White Rice
Serving Size	45g	42g	47g
Calories	170	150	170
NUTRIENTS			
Total fat (g)	0g	1g	0g
Saturated fat (g)	0g	0g	0g
Cholesterol	0mg	0mg	0mg
Sodium (mg)	0mg	0mg	0mg
Total Carbohydrate (g)	35g	32g	37g
Dietary fiber (g)	2g	1g	0g
Sugars (g)	0g	0g	0g
Protein (g)	6g	3g	4g
VITAMINS AND MINERALS*			
Vitamin A (%DV)	2%	0%	0%
Vitamin C (%DV)	0%	0%	0%
Niacin (%DV)	15%	6%	8%
Calcium (%DV)	2%	0%	0%
Iron (%DV)	4%	6%	8%

* %DV = Percent Daily Values based on 2,000 calorie diet

In general, "The composition of the wild rice grain resembles that of oats. The protein percent is high and the fat percentage low compared to other cereals" (*Wild Rice Production in Minnesota*, Extension Bulletin 464, 1982, E.A. Oelke, page 37). Oelke also states that scarification of wild rice "during processing does not result in much loss of minerals."

Gluten: The gluten content of wild rice has not been determined. However, many people who are allergic to gluten seem to be able to eat wild rice with no adverse reaction.

Adapted from *Wild Rice Facts,* Gourmet House, Clearbrook, Minnesota. Used with permission.

stored in birch bark containers not only through the winter following harvest, but into subsequent winters.

Wild rice is still a staple in pantries in "wild rice country." It is as likely to show up in a casserole at a potluck dinner as in a dressing at a holiday feast. Because of its popularity there, it is sold not only in large grocery stores, but at mini-groceries, retail stores, restaurants, and even at service stations.

From the beginning, wild rice found its way out of the western Great Lakes area in the food stores of traveling American Indians, and through trade with other tribes and explorers, traders and settlers. But it was not until the 1960s, with the advent of cultivated paddies, first in Minnesota and then in California, that it became consistently available nationwide. Wild rice from natural stands in the western Great Lakes area currently account for only five million of the thirty-three million pounds of raw wild rice harvested annually.[1]

Lake Rice, River Rice, Cultivated (Paddy) Rice

For as long as stories have been told, the rice growing in certain lake or river stands has been considered better eating than the rice from other stands. Some connoisseurs also argue the gastronomic qualities of river rice over lake rice, and vice versa. And don't even get them started on the difference in taste between naturally occurring rice and cultivated rice.

Rice experts report that "wild rice grown on different stands is sufficiently different so that an experienced buyer can often tell where it came from by looking at it."[2] In addition, it is generally accepted that the flavor of wild rice is also affected by how green or mature it is when it is harvested, and by processing methods.[3]

Before I researched this book, I used to stand in the aisle at the grocery and stare at my wild rice options. Black and thick; brown and thinner; cultivated; machine-harvested; hand-harvested. Which one was best? I had hoped to answer this question in the course of my research and, in a way, I did. I discovered that the question is not "which one is best?" but "which one do I like best, and which one is best for the use I have in mind?"

Rice from each of three major growing milieus has generally predictable physical features: U.S. lake and river rice tends to be thin and short; Canadian lake and river rice tends to be thin and long; and cultivated rice tends to be thick and short, with California cultivated rice being a bit thicker and shorter than Minnesota cultivated rice. However, these qualities do not affect flavor as much as they affect cooking time: longer and thicker grains take longer to cook than thinner and shorter grains.

The method of processing has more impact on the flavor of wild rice than its source or its size, for it is the processing that determines the amount of bran

Table II	A Buyer's Guide: *Look at the Rice*

Black wild rice has most of the bran layer intact. It usually cooks in 45 to 60 minutes, and has a distinct smoky, nutty, wild rice flavor. Its slightly chewy texture is similar to that of ordinary brown rice.

Brown wild rice has some of the bran layer removed, or "scarified." It usually cooks in 30 to 45 minutes, has a milder nutty, smoky wild rice flavor, and is softer in texture than black wild rice.

Blond wild rice has most of the bran removed, and cooks in 10 to 15 minutes. It has a light smoky, nutty wild rice flavor, and is delicate in texture.

Long wild rice (⅝ to ⅞ inch) usually comes from Canada and is usually black in color. It cooks in 45 to 60 minutes.

Medium length wild rice (⅜ to ½ inch) is the length of most U.S. wild rice. It may be black or brown in color, and sometimes blond.

Broken wild rice (⅛ to ¼ inch) Broken wild rice is less expensive than whole rice. Because of the different sizes of the bits, it often cooks unevenly, usually in 15 to 25 minutes. It is appropriate for baked goods, or other dishes where a well-cooked rice is desirable, and is excellent for popping.

Note: The color of wild rice is determined by scarification of the bran layer during processing. See color insert for illustrations on color and size.

left on the kernels. It is the bran, for the most part, that determines the flavor. Wild rice with the bran intact is black in color and its flavor has a pungent edge to it, considered desirable by most people, but not by all. It takes forty-five to sixty minutes to cook. Brown rice, with most of the bran intact, is milder and usually takes thirty to forty minutes to cook. Blond rice, with most of the bran removed, is extremely mild and almost sweet in flavor. It is usually best cooked by pouring boiling water over it and allowing it to steep for ten to fifteen minutes.

Buying Wild Rice

The "best" wild rice is the one that suits the needs of the cook. Tables III, IV, and V will help you understand the cooking requirements, and taste and texture results of the rich variety of wild rice products.

Today, many larger grocery stores carry one-hundred percent wild rice, and most carry "value added" wild rice products. These include wild and white rice blends, dried soup mixes, and rice cakes.

For Internet shoppers, a world of wild rice products is available at the click of a mouse. Search for "wild rice" using your favorite Web search engine. Most sites also offer a toll-free phone number for ordering.

Cooking Wild Rice

The only hard thing about cooking wild rice is knowing when it's done, and that is easy to learn: it is done when most of the kernels are split open to reveal the white inside, and a few of the kernels have "butterflied," or opened all the way and are peeled back. It will be tender yet still a bit chewy.

To cook wild rice, simmer it in water or broth until it is done, usually in thirty to sixty minutes depending on its type.

If all of the water is not absorbed when the rice is done, either pour it off or, if the rice can stand a few more minutes of cooking, boil it off. Let the finished rice stand off the heat for ten to fifteen minutes and then fluff it with a fork.

Table III	A Buyer's Guide: *Look at the Label*

Note: Labels sometimes give the origin of the rice, and the method of harvesting. However, the method of *processing* affects the qualities of the finished rice more than do the origin site or the harvesting method.

Hand-harvested or traditionally harvested wild rice is always from western Great Lakes area rivers or lakes and is harvested by canoe.

Lake or river wild rice grows naturally in lakes or rivers. If it is also Minnesota or Wisconsin rice, it is hand-harvested. Canadian lake and river rice is usually harvested by airboat.

Machine harvested wild rice may be from cultivated paddies in the United States, or from naturally occurring paddies in Canada.

Cultivated or paddy rice will be from cultivated paddies in the United States. Currently most wild rice is grown in paddies in Minnesota and California, and sometimes in Wisconsin and Oregon.

100% wild rice indicates that the package is not a blend of wild rice with white or brown rice.

100% pure wild rice is a descriptive label and does not indicate organic certification. It is sometimes used for lake and river rice, which are not fertilized or treated with pesticides. It is also used for some cultivated rice that is not treated with pesticides.

Certified Organic wild rice has been approved by an organic foods association. It usually means that no pesticides or fertilizers have been used on the rice stands for at least three years.

Minnesota, California, Canada, Oregon, Wisconsin, or other place names indicate site of origin of the rice in the package. Some marketers also use local place names, such as "Leech Lake," in Minnesota.

Minnesota Labeling Laws require that labels on wild rice sold in Minnesota prominently display the place of origin of the rice, and the method of harvesting.
California Grade Regulations offer standardized grading for California wild rice, based on the size and length of the kernels: Large, Medium, Thin, Short, Broken, and Mixed.
Marketer's Categories are created by some marketers and processors. They indicate standardized in-house categories for their own products, such as "House Blend" and "Fancy."
Quick-cooking or instant wild rice has been precooked and dehydrated so that it can be rehydrated quickly by the consumer. It has a mild flavor, and rice usually cooks in 3 to 10 minutes.
Wild rice flour is made from finely ground processed wild rice and can be substituted for part of the flour in baked goods. Recipes and instructions usually come with the package. It is available from some specialty marketers.

It is alright to check wild rice while it is cooking, and you can stir it if you want to. In fact, if you are new to wild rice, it is a good idea to start checking it about half way through the cooking time, and then every ten minutes after that, so you don't overcook it. It's overcooked when all the kernels are butterflied. Overcooked wild rice is soft and disintegrates easily. It is, however, ideal for adding to baked goods, such as pancakes and bread.

The best way to get good at cooking wild rice is to do it often. Try different kinds of rice and decide which one you like best.

Table IV	WILD RICE YIELDS
1 cup uncooked yields 3 to 4 cups cooked.	
1 pound uncooked yields 8 to 10 cups cooked.	
1 pound uncooked equals 2¾ cups uncooked.	
At $5.00 per pound, one pound uncooked yields 16 to 20 one-half-cup cooked servings, at 25 cents to 31 cents per serving.	

Table V	APPROXIMATE WILD RICE COOKING TIMES
(Also see Table II: A Buyer's Guide to Wild Rice)	
Black wild rice	45 to 60 minutes
Brown wild rice	30 to 45 minutes
Blond wild rice	10 to 20 minutes
Quick or instant wild rice	3 to 10 minutes
Broken wild rice	15 to 25 minutes
Note: After you have cooked and eaten wild rice a few times, you will discover your personal preference for color, flavor, texture, and doneness.	

Table VI	COOKING INSTRUCTIONS

Basic Stovetop Instructions	**Yield:** Multiply amount of uncooked rice by 3 or 4 (1 cup rice yields 3 to 4 cups cooked rice).
	
	3 parts water or broth
	1 part wild rice
	$^1/_2$ teaspoon salt per cup of rice (Optional: omit if using salted broth.)
	
	Rinse the rice in a strainer. In a kettle appropriate to the amount of rice being cooked, bring the water, rice, and salt to a boil. Reduce heat, cover, and simmer until done, when kernels are split open, revealing the white inside. Some will be "butterflied"— opened and peeled back. It will be tender yet still a bit chewy. Black wild rice will usually cook in 40 to 60 minutes. Brown wild rice will usually cook in 30 to 45 minutes.
	    It is all right to remove the lid during cooking to check on the rice. Stir if desired. Add more water or broth if necessary.
	    When the rice is done, excess liquid can be drained or boiled off. Wild rice fluffs up nicely when allowed to sit for ten or fifteen minutes and then stirred with a fork.

Basic Microwave Instructions	Using 1 cup of rice and 3 cups of water, cook as for stovetop. Use an 8 cup glass container. Use "high" setting for 5 minutes, then reduce to 50 or a medium or simmer setting. Cook for the same amount of time as on the stovetop, and add 10 to 15 minutes standing time.
Basic Oven Instructions	Cook as for stovetop except start with boiling water, use a covered casserole dish, and bake at 375°F.

Instructions for blond wild rice	Blond wild rice is heavily scarified, which means most of the bran has been removed. It should not be boiled or simmered. Instead, measure out 3 parts water to 1 part rice (same as for black and brown wild rice). Bring the water to a boil, then pour it over the rice. Cover and let sit without heat for 10 to 20 minutes. The rice will be delicate in flavor and texture. It should be eaten as is; mixing it with other foods will likely cause it to break down.

Eat it straight or use it in a recipe

Cooked wild rice is delicious with a little butter, salt, and pepper. Most recipes that use wild rice call for it to be cooked, so when you simmer up a batch, make plenty and freeze the extra.

Freezing Cooked Wild Rice

Frozen, cooked wild rice works in recipes just as well as freshly cooked wild rice. Store extra cooked rice in the freezer in one or two cup portions. It thaws quickly in the microwave, or in a bowl of hot water in the sink.

Frozen, cooked wild rice is good fast food. It makes a gourmet dish out of other leftovers: add it to soups, stuffings, beans, stir-frys, pancakes, and omelets. Or serve it as a simple side dish garnished with butter, salt, and pepper.

Parboiling and Presoaking Wild Rice

Wild rice can be soaked ahead of time or parboiled (pour boiling water over the rice and let it sit for an hour or so), but neither method decreases cooking time by more than five or ten minutes or improves the quality of the finished rice.

Storing Cooked Wild Rice

Cooked rice can be kept in the fridge for a couple of weeks, or in the freezer indefinitely.

Storing Uncooked Wild Rice

Uncooked rice should be kept in a sealed container in a cool, dry place. It is not necessary to freeze it, and it should not be kept in the fridge, which is usually a moist environment. Wild rice that is kept in a closed container usually keeps indefinitely in the cupboard.

Make Extra

When cooking wild rice, make a double or triple batch (a one pound bag makes eight to ten cups cooked) and freeze the extra in one-cup portions. Cooking larger batches on the stovetop or in the oven does not alter the cooking time. Large batches do not pay off in the microwave: doing more than one cup of uncooked rice at a time takes longer than doing a large batch on the stovetop or in the oven.

It's *Not* Expensive!

Remember that wild rice is economical. At current retail prices, that's about 25 to 30 cents per one-half-cup serving. A $5.00 one-pound bag of rice will make sixteen to twenty half-cup servings.

❊ Breads and Breakfast ❊

Breads

Bread Machine Wild Rice Wheat Bread   30
Savory Meal in a Muffin   31
Tony's Wild Rice Muffins   32
Wild Rice Sandwich Buns   33

Breakfast

Quick Wild Rice Pancakes and Waffles   34
Sour Cream Wild Rice Pancakes   34
Wild Rice Whole Wheat Pancakes   35
Applesauce Wild Rice Crepes   35
Wild Rice "As Is" Breakfast Cereal   36
Wild Rice and Eggs Breakfast Bake   37

Breads

 ## Bread Machine Wild Rice Wheat Bread
From the kitchen of Andrew and Debbie Warne-Jacobsen.

This recipe can also be made the old-fashioned way—in a food processor or by hand.

¾ cup plus 2 tablespoons water

1 tablespoon margarine

1 tablespoon brown sugar

1¼ cup wheat flour

¾ cup white flour

½ cup cooked wild rice (page 26)

1 teaspoon salt

1¼ teaspoon yeast

Place ingredients in order into the loaf pan. Select the wheat and small loaf settings.

Savory Meal in a Muffin

From the kitchen of Carol Jessen-Klixbull.

2 cups flour
1 tablespoon baking powder
1 cup buttermilk
$\frac{1}{2}$ cup vegetable oil
2 large eggs
1 cup cooked wild rice (page 26)
¾ cup shredded cheese
1 cup ham, diced*
$\frac{1}{2}$ medium onion, finely chopped
2 tablespoons fresh cilantro, finely chopped**

Preheat oven to 400°F. Grease 18 cups of 2½-inch muffin pans or line pans with paper baking cups. Combine flour and baking powder in a large bowl. In a small bowl, whisk together the buttermilk, oil, and eggs. Stir liquid ingredients into dry ingredients just until combined. Fold in the wild rice, cheese, ham, onion, and cilantro. Spoon into prepared muffin cups, filling each about three quarters full. Bake for 15 to 20 minutes or until toothpick inserted in center of muffin comes out clean. Cool in pans on wire racks for 5 minutes. Remove from pans and serve warm. Muffins may be cooled completely, wrapped well and frozen for up to one month. To reheat, loosely wrap each muffin in a paper towel and microwave on high for 15 to 20 seconds.

*One-fourth pound of crisply fried, crumbled bacon can be substituted for the ham. **Parsley or another favorite herb could be used instead of the cilantro.

Makes 18 muffins.

Serving suggestions: Serve with a fresh green salad and fresh fruit for a light lunch. Or the muffins are good by themselves for a filling snack.

Tony's Wild Rice Muffins
From the kitchen of MacDougall's California Wild Rice, Marysville, California.

1 cup cooked wild rice (page 26)
3 eggs, lightly beaten
7 tablespoons oil
1 cup milk
1¼ cups whole wheat flour
1 tablespoon baking powder
½ teaspoon salt
2 tablespoons sugar
½ cup chopped walnuts

Stir wild rice with eggs, oil, and milk. Mix flour, baking powder, salt, and sugar. Stir liquid ingredients into dry, mixing thoroughly. Stir in walnuts and spoon batter into paper muffin cups. Bake at 425°F for 15 to 18 minutes or until muffins are lightly browned.

Makes 12 muffins.

Wild Rice Sandwich Buns
From the kitchen of the author.

These delicious buns go from scratch to table in about 90 minutes. Perfect for Sunday evening sandwiches made with leftover beef or chicken.

½ cup warm water (105–115°F)
2 packages active dry yeast
¾ cup milk, warmed to 105–115°F
1 teaspoon salt
¼ cup sugar
¼ cup (½ stick) butter or margarine
1 egg
3½ cups unsifted flour
1 cup cooked wild rice (page 26)

Put warm water in a 1-cup measure and add yeast, stirring until dissolved; let sit a few minutes. Warm milk (in microwave or on stove); stir in salt, sugar, and butter or margarine. Put milk mixture in a large bowl. Add egg, flour, yeast mixture, and wild rice; stir to make a soft dough. Cover. Let rise about 30 minutes or until doubled in bulk. Punch down and shape into 12 round buns. Place on a greased baking sheet. Cover; let rise in a warm, draft-free place until doubled in bulk, about 30 minutes. Bake in a 400°F oven for about 15 minutes.

Makes 12 buns.

Breakfast

QUICK WILD RICE PANCAKES AND WAFFLES

Add cooked wild rice (page 26) to your favorite pancake or waffle batter, about 1 cup of wild rice to 1½ cups of flour.

 ## Sour Cream Wild Rice Pancakes
From the kitchen of Nancy Lee-Borden.

---

1 egg, beaten
1 cup milk
2 tablespoons sour cream
1 cup cooked wild rice (page 26)
2 tablespoons butter, melted
1 cup flour
½ teaspoon salt
1 tablespoon baking powder
1 tablespoon sugar

Beat together the egg, milk, and sour cream. Stir in wild rice and butter. Sift together flour, salt, baking powder, sugar, and stir into egg and rice mixture until smooth. Cook as for regular pancakes.

Makes 9 three-inch pancakes.

Wild Rice Whole Wheat Pancakes
From the kitchen of MacDougall's California Wild Rice, Marysville, California.

4 eggs, separated
⅓ cup buttermilk
1 cup cooked wild rice (page 26)
⅔ cup whole wheat flour
1 tablespoon sugar
½ teaspoon salt
½ teaspoon baking powder
1 teaspoon vanilla
1 tablespoon oil

Beat together egg yolks, buttermilk, wild rice, flour, sugar, salt, baking powder, vanilla, and oil. In another bowl, beat egg whites until stiff but not dry. Fold the beaten whites gently into the wild rice mixture. Drop batter by large spoonfuls onto an oiled skillet or griddle. Pancakes should be golden brown on both sides, and puffy. Serve immediately, topped with fresh fruit and yogurt or maple syrup.

 ## Applesauce Wild Rice Crepes
From the kitchen of MacDougall's California Wild Rice, Marysville, California.

1 cup all-purpose flour
¼ teaspoon salt

1 1/2 teaspoon baking powder
1/2 cup milk
1 egg
1 tablespoon melted butter or oil
1/2 teaspoon vanilla
1 1/4 cups applesauce, preferably homemade
1/2 cup cooked wild rice (page 26)

Sift dry ingredients together in mixing bowl. Stir in milk, eggs, butter or oil, vanilla, applesauce, and rice. Beat well, then spoon batter onto a hot, greased griddle, making pancakes about 4 inches in diameter. When the edges are lightly browned, turn and bake on other side. Serve for breakfast with maple syrup, or as a dessert with warmed honey, melted apple jelly, and whipped cream.

 ## Wild Rice "As Is" Breakfast Cereal
From the kitchen of Margaret H. Harlow.

Cooked wild rice (page 26)
Melted butter
Brown sugar
Cream or milk

Stir melted butter into warm or cold wild rice. Top with brown sugar and cream or milk and serve as breakfast cereal.

Wild Rice and Eggs Breakfast Bake
From the kitchen of Nancy R. Kapp.

3 cups cooked wild rice (page 26)
2 cups cooked ham, cubed
2 tablespoons butter
1 dozen eggs, lightly beaten
⅓ cup milk
3 tablespoons butter
1½ pound broccoli cooked until just tender
Cheese sauce (see below)

Put rice in greased 9x13-inch baking dish. Sauté ham in butter. Place ham and pan juices on top of wild rice. Combine eggs with milk. Melt 3 tablespoons butter in skillet and scramble eggs just until soft. Spoon eggs onto ham in baking dish. Place broccoli down center of baking dish. Spoon cheese sauce over all. Bake covered at 325°F for 25 minutes; uncover and bake another 10 to 15 minutes uncovered.

Serves 8 to 10.

Cheese Sauce
2 tablespoons oil
3 tablespoons flour
1 cup milk

2 cups grated cheese
⅛ teaspoon pepper
Salt to taste

Heat oil in skillet and stir in flour. Add milk. Cook and stir until sauce thickens slightly. Stir in cheese; add pepper and salt.

T H R E E

Manoomin

The Ojibwe call wild rice *manoomin* (*muh-NOO-min* or *muh-NOE-min*). The word is similar to their word for corn, *mandaamin*. The prefix *man* (pronounced "mahn") has qualities of wonder, which include the English word "good." The suffix *min* means "grainlike" or "berrylike." The middle of both words describes the fruit: *oo* designates "kernel," *daa* designates "hard stalk," or "club-shaped stalk," as in the corn cob. *Manoomin* means "good, kernellike berry"; *mandaamin* means "good, clublike berry."[1]

In English, *manoomin* is spelled many ways. Warren Upham relates some of them in his book *Minnesota Geographic Names*. In "The Song of Hiawatha,"

Longfellow spells it *Mahnomonee.* In Minnesota and Wisconsin we find rivers, lakes, towns, cities, and counties whose names reflect similar variations: *mahnomen, manomin, menomonee, menomonie, menominee. Menominee* is also the name of the Wisconsin American Indian tribe traditionally known as the wild rice people.[2]

The term "rice" is not part of the Ojibwe name for *manoomin.* Wild rice got its contemporary, common English name from the Europeans who compared the *manoomin* kernel to that of *Oryza sativa,* what we know as common white rice. In the taxonomic system, wild rice and ordinary rice are placed in the same order and family, *Graminales,* and *Gramineae,* respectively. But from there they split off, wild rice into the tribe *Zizanieae,* and rice into *Oryzeae.*

Before the English name wild rice took hold in our vocabulary, *manoomin* was known by other common names. The first Europeans to frequent the western Great Lakes country of North America called it "wild oats," because the plant itself closely resembles European oats. Other common names include Indian oats, blackbird oats, black rice, and Canadian rice.[3] The French explorers called it *folles avoine,* "false" or "wild oats." Today the French call it *riz sauvage,* a direct translation of "wild rice."

The early visitors to the new world who dubbed *manoomin* with terms relating it to oats were right on track, for the wild rice grain has an amino acid profile similar to oats. However, Dr. E. A. Oelke, University of Minnesota Professor of Agronomy and Plant Genetics, reports that recent gene mapping research by Dr. Ronald Phillips, University of Minnesota, found that some of the markers used to locate genes in rice can also be used to locate genes in wild rice chromosomes.[4] This raises some questions as to the specific origin of wild rice: perhaps it is more closely related to rice than previously believed. Still, depending on where in Central America the line is drawn between North and South America, *manoomin* can be called the only indigenous grain in North America.

The variety of commonplace names for *manoomin* carries over to the scientific world, where the dimension of outright confusion is added. While from the beginning botanists recognized *manoomin* as a grain, it has taken several centuries to come to an accurate taxonomic classification.

The trouble started long ago, in 1753, when Carolus Linnaeus, founder of the modern classification system for plants and animals, classified wild rice. He put it in a new genus, *Zizania.*[5] *Zizania* is the Greek plural of Lolium, the Biblical name for a common oatlike weed. But it was not this genus name that led to confusion; it was the naming of the species, *aquatica.* One researcher, Lawrence Hoff, explains the problem: "Linnaeus had based *Zizania aquatica* on the southern specimen while he described the northern version. . . . Linnaeus's reference obviously belongs to one plant while his specimen belongs to another." Hoff goes on to describe the 1908 correction to the problem with the identification of two *Zizania* species, *aquatica* and *palustris, palustris* meaning "swamp-dwelling."[6]

In the almost one hundred years since then, wild rice has remained in the original taxonomic order, *Graminales,* and family, *Gramineae,* and the genus *Zizania* assigned by Linnaeus. However, the species names have undergone a series of modifications, mostly based on the advancement of scientific processes. Today, with the aid of such techniques as electrophoretic enzyme analysis, the species of wild rice have probably come to their final resting place in taxonomy.[7]

A summary of this final classification is included in the pamphlet "Wild Rice: New Interest in an Old Crop." Here we discover that there are four species of wild rice, of which three, *aquatica, palustris,* and *texana,* occur indigenously only in North America. The fourth, *latifolia* ("large-leaved") is indigenous only to Manchuria, Korea, Japan, Burma, and northeastern India.[8] *Z. aquatica* and *Z. palustris* are annuals. *Z. texana* and *Z. latifolia* are perennials. Of the four, only *Z. palustris,* with its larger, fuller seed, is suitable for humans to eat. The seed of the others is meager by comparison, although the many birds that thrive on it do not seem to mind. While *Z. latifolia* seeds are

Wild rice is an important food for wild life, especially birds. This migrating sora rail, *Porzana carolina,* is feeding on the abundant seeds of *Zizania aquatica* in the wildlife marsh in the Patuxent River Park, Maryland. Photo courtesy naturalist Greg Kearns, Patuxent River Park, Maryland National-Capital Park and Planning Commission.

Table VII	DESCRIPTION AND DISTRIBUTION OF *ZIZANIA* SPECIES
E.A. Oelke et al, "Wild Rice: New Interest in an Old Crop," *Cereal Foods World,* April 1997, Vol. 42, No. 4. Used with permission.	
Zizania aquatica var. aquatica L. southern wild rice	Annual plants 180–240 cm tall; stalk often cm thick at base; leaf blades 2.5–5.0 cm wide, pale green, usually drooping outward at top; panicles large, usually 50 cm long, many branched with numerous florets; pistillate florets with an awn usually 2.5–7.5 cm long. Hull of grain thin, papery, dull, and minutely roughened on the surface. Found on muddy shores of streams in southern Ontario and Quebec, southward to Florida and Louisiana.
Zizania aquatica var. brevis, Fasset, estuarine wild rice	Annual plants 30–90 cm tall, with slender flexible stalks; leaf blades usually less than 1.5 cm wide, dull green. Panicles usually 10–25 cm long, few branched and with few florets. Pistillate florets with awns less than 1.2 cm long. Hull of grain thin, papery, dull, and minutely roughened on the surface. Found on tidal flats of St. Lawrence River estuary.
Zizania palustris var. palustris L., northern wild rice	Annual plants 90–240 cm tall; stems usually extending 60–120 cm above the water surface, rather slender; leaf blades 1–2 cm wide; panicle slender and few-flowered, the staminate florets usually numbering less than 15 on a branch, the pistillate usually only two to six on a branch. Hull of the grain firm and leathery, shiny and smooth on the surface but scabrous in the furrows. Found in water up to 120 cm deep. Widespread in southern Canada from New Brunswick to Manitoba and in the northern states of the United States.

Zizania palustris var. interior (Fassett) Dore, interior wild rice	Annual plants 120–240 cm tall; leaf blades 1.2–3.6 cm wide; panicles ample, branches generally divergent and many-flowered, the staminate florets numbering over 30 on a branch, the pistillate 10–30 on a branch. Hull of the grain firm and leathery, shiny and smooth on the surface but scabrous in the furrows. Found on muddy shores and in water up to 30 cm deep along rivers in southeastern Manitoba and adjoining Ontario and abundant in the North Central States.
Zizania texana A.S., Hitchc., Texas wild rice	Perennial plants with 50 or more decumbant stems that can be over 360 cm long. Roots develop at nodes of decumbant stems; basel area of clone rangers from a few to over 300 cm^2; leaves are bright green, ribbonlike, 2.5 cm wide, and can exceed 180 cm in length; panicles 20–30 cm long; panicle characteristics similar to those of *Z. aquatica* var. aquatica, but seeds much shorter. Found in localized areas in San Marcos River in Texas.
Zizania latifolia Turcz., Manchurian water-rice	Perennial plants, spreading by coarse subterranean runners. Staminate and pistillate florets borne on stems having hairs at tips, a corresponding crown of hairs present on the base of the hull of the floret. Hull of the grain thin, papery, dull, and rough. A native grass of Manchuria, Korea, Japan, Burma, and northeastern India. Base of the plant often becomes infected with fungus, which is used as a food delicacy.

not used as food (they are often too small and thin), the whitish base of the plant, when it is infected with a certain fungus (*Ustilago esculenta* P. Henn.), is considered a food delicacy in the Asian areas where it grows. It is called

Makomo-take in Japanese and *Chiao pei* or *Gau sun* in Chinese, and tastes something like a cross between bamboo shoots and asparagus.[9]

In general, of the North American species, *Z. aquatica* grows on the East Coast from Canada down to Florida, and on the Gulf Coast. *Z. palustris,* the species used for human food, grows inland in most of the north and eastern United States and in south central Canada. *Z. texana* grows in localized areas of the San Marcos river in Texas.

Because these classifications are fairly recent, it is still common to see the food wild rice identified as *Z. aquatica,* especially in articles in popular literature. However, all such wild rice is *Z. palustris,* including that now grown in cultivated paddies in its native areas and in California and Oregon. Barb Carstens, Executive Secretary for the International Wild Rice Association,

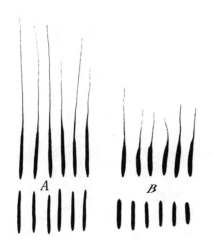

The seeds of item A, *Zizania aquatica* are considerably longer and thinner than those of item B, which today would be identified as *Z. palustris.* While both species are important foods for wild life, only the more robust *Z. palustris* is harvested for human use. From the original caption, Plate 59: "A, Dried seeds of the broad-leaved form *(Z. aquatica)* from Arlington County, Va., in upper row unhulled, in lower, hulled. B, Dried seeds of the narrow-leaved form *(Z. a.* var. augustifolia) originating from northern stock but grown in Mason County, Ill." Martin, A.D. and F.M. Uhler. Food and Game Ducks in the United States and Canada. USDA Technical Bulletin 634, 1939.

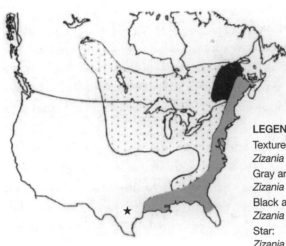

Distribution of wild rice in North America. E.A. Oelke et al, "Wild Rice-New Interest in an Old Crop," *Cereal Foods World*, April 1997. Adapted from USDA Technical Bulletin 634, 1939. Used with permission.

LEGEND

Textured area:
Zizania palustris varieties palustris and interior

Gray area:
Zizania aquatica variety aquatica

Black area:
Zizania aquatica variety brevis

Star:
Zizania texana

reported in 1998 that *Z. palustris* has also been cultivated in Idaho, and that it is currently being produced in Australia and Hungary.[10] Cultivated wild rice experiments have been carried out in Florida.[11]

The three North American species of *Zizania* share certain requirements for growth. They are all water plants, and in general they grow in the same way, and their flower panicles look alike. In the spring they emerge from the bottom of the lake or river. By mid- to late summer they emerge from the water, and they flower and go to seed by the end of summer. However, within those parameters the plants are wonderfully varied.

Z. palustris insists on soft, mucky ground. In the spring, seeds that fell the previous autumn germinate and begin their stretch toward air. If the water they are in is stagnant, they will not be satisfied with its nutritional content. If it is turbulent, as in a rapidly flowing river, the seedlings will easily dislodge and be destroyed. *Z. palustris,* then, is found in lakes and swamps that have some flowage, in small, lazy creeks, and in the side waters of larger rivers.

In the spring, if you are in a canoe on a river in northern Minnesota, and you look down and see single, slender leaves from a few to many inches long flowing with the current, you are probably looking at wild rice. If you come back midsummer, you will find the same plants have grown to the water's surface, and are beginning to emerge from it. Air cells between divisions in the plant's stem help it to remain upright.

If you return in another month or so, the plants will have grown two to three feet above the water, and will be in flower. All *Zizania* species carry both the male and female flowers on each plant. The female flowers are on the topmost part of the stalk and emerge from the stalk before the male flowers which are on the same stalk. This helps to ensure that the plants will be fertilized by the pollen from different plants.

Table VIII	GROWTH CYCLE OF *ZIZANIA PALUSTRIS*
April–May	Germination, first growth, and floating leaf
June	Emergence from the water
July	Flowering
August–September	Grain formation and seed maturation

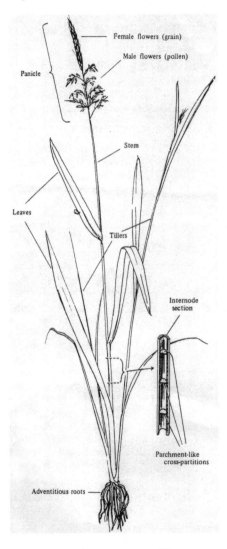

Zizania palustris, "Commercial Production of Wild Rice," E. A. Oelke, et al. Agricultural Extension Service, University of Minnesota, undated. Used with permission.

If you visit the wild rice stand in late August or early September, depending on the year, the plants may have grown three to four feet above the water and the female flowers may have given way to seed. You can tell by gently shaking the stalk. If the seeds are ripe, they will easily fall off the stalks, called "shattering." If they do, you will also notice that the immature seeds stay on the plant. Wild rice seeds ripen over a period of time. Most wild rice completes its ripening in ten to fourteen days.

The seeds that are released into the water sink almost immediately to the bottom of the lake or river, where barbed awns on their hulls pull them down into the mud. They lie dormant throughout the winter, and in the spring, when the water begins to warm, they germinate and begin the cycle again. The kernels from one year's crop are seed for the next year's crop, or sometimes for succeeding years. Seeds that do not germinate but stay wet or moist can remain viable for at least another year.

This cold and wet dormancy period is necessary for germination of *Z. palustris*. Without it, the seeds lose their viability. *Z. palustris*, as with all of the *Zizania* species, is also fussy about the water it grows in. It requires a mineral-rich environment, and does not tolerate pollutants.[12]

Z. palustris also requires water of a certain depth, six inches to three feet.[13] Water levels outside those parameters are not usually conducive to wild rice growth. And water level changes within a growing season can damage a crop: water that is too low will not support a stalk that has grown tall, and water that is too high can drown a developed plant.[14]

Z. palustris seeds range from about one-third inch in length to one inch, depending on the variety and on the growing conditions. In general, the northern variety, which grows mostly in Canada, has a longer seed than the interior Minnesota and Wisconsin variety.

Z. aquatica is the eastern cousin of *Z. palustris*. The plants look alike except that the female flower heads of *Z. aquatica* tend to splay out while those in *Z. palustris* stay gathered against the stem. The hull of the *Z. aquatica* seed carries the same barbed awn as *Z. palustris,* but the seed tends to be thin and long, up to about one inch. Its meager kernel is the reason it is not harvested for human food.

Z. aquatica flourishes today in gently flowing, nutrient-rich East Coast tidal marshes.[15] There the plants grow eight to twelve feet above the water, well beyond the *Z. palustris* usual height of three to four feet. Both plants require a wet dormancy, but *Z. aquatica* does not require the near-freezing conditions necessary for *Z. palustris*.

Z. palustris and *Z. aquatica* share several traits not shared by their cousin *Z. texana*. They are annuals, reproducing from seed, and they insist on nutrient-rich, quiet water that is kept fresh by gentle flowage. *Z. texana* is a perennial, reproducing from its roots, and it thrives in rapidly moving water. In fact, the wild rice is more productive in the higher flow areas of the San Marcos River, which is the only place it currently grows.[16]

As with the *Z. aquatica* species of the eastern U.S. and Canada, *Z. texana* has a thin seed that is of interest only to wildlife. It grows as tall as *Z. aquatica*, even getting as tall as fifteen feet.[17] However, most of that growth is submerged in the rapid waters of the San Marcos. The flowering parts of the plant rise only twelve to eighteen inches above the water. The seeds of *Z. texana* are the smallest of the three North American species, normally growing to only one-quarter to one-half inch in length. The seeds are not important in reproduction as the plant regenerates from shoots sent out from its base.

The wild rice in the San Marcos River has been the subject of much environmental concern. The river is heavily used for recreation, including boating and tubing. Both activities disturb and even destroy the few wild rice stands still viable in the river; *Z. texana* has been declared an endangered species, and efforts are underway to preserve it and its habitat.[18]

Z. aquatica and *Z. palustris* also suffer from the encroachment of civilization, both from water pollution and from loss of habitat to development. As with most environmental problems, the concerns go beyond the loss of the plants themselves. *Z. aquatica* is a major East Coast food source for resident and migrating birds and ducks.[19] The same is true inland for *Z. palustris.* And not only the seeds are of value: All parts of the plant are eaten by ducks and other waterfowl, and many birds and other animals also use the wild rice stands for shelter.[20]

It is not known for certain if fish, especially carp, have a positive or negative effect on wild rice. They may uproot some plants with their foraging, but with the same action, they also help loosen soil that has become too compact to support wild rice. Muskrats, the only mammal besides humans that impacts wild rice, also play a dual role. The building of dams sometimes contributes to the development of swamps where wild rice can grow, and sometimes causes flooding in stands that are already established.[21]

Wild rice is sometimes plagued by cutworms, aphids, and other insects, can be affected by a fungus, and can be retarded in growth by the excessive presence of algae in the water.[22] Excessive algae can be caused by runoff from agricultural fields and other human practices.

It is easy to understand how wild rice was spread throughout the swamp- and marsh-friendly areas of North America through the beneficence of the birds and ducks that are so appreciative of its value. We know, too, that American Indians cultivated wild rice by sowing it in appropriate areas where it was not already growing, and by reseeding beds that needed replenishing.[23]

Neither of these activities, however, explain the presence of *Zizania* on the Asian continent. Like *Z. texana,* it is a perennial. Like *Z. texana* and *Z. aquatica,* its seed is thin and not usable as a harvested food. *Zizania* is not the only plant that shares this geographic diversity. Poison ivy, of the *Toxicodendron* genus, is also found only in North America and in parts of Asia, including Japan.

This "disrupted distribution," says Moyle in his 1969 report, is shared by a number of other plants, including "the tulip tree, sassafras, moonseed, . . . blue cohosh, and May apple." He speculates that "they are remnants of an ancient—probably Cretaceous—flora that once had a continuous distribution but which now has this disrupted pattern." Moyle concludes that ". . . wild rice is an ancient kind of grass that antedates man and his ability to distribute it by planting. Although Indians may have, and probably did, plant some North American stands, the original distribution must have come about in some other way."[24]

❊ Salads and Soups ❊

Salads

Curried Chicken or Shrimp Wild Rice Salad   56
Sweet and Tasty Wild Rice Salad   57
Warm and Nutty Wild Rice Salad   57
Tarragon and Chicken Wild Rice Salad   58
Wild Rice Garlic Chicken Salad   59
Wild Rice Salad with Hard-Cooked Eggs   60
Wild Rice and Bean Salad   61

Soups

Wild Rice Fast Food Soup   62
Karen's Overnight Cream of Wild Rice Soup   62
Cream of Wild Rice Soup with Bacon   63
Cream of Potato and Wild Rice Soup   63
Cream of Wild Rice Soup with Sherry   64
Quick Wild Rice and Black Bean Soup   65
Wild Rice Broth Soup   66
Sherried Wild Rice Soup   67

Salads

Curried Chicken or Shrimp Wild Rice Salad

From the kitchen of Gretchen Pinsonneault.

1½ cups cooked wild rice (page 26)

2 cups cooked chicken breast or cooked shrimp

1 can sliced water chestnuts

1 can artichoke hearts in water

2 cups grapes or 2 small cans mandarin oranges

1 cup pecans

5 green onions

Dressing

1 cup mayonnaise (Hellman's preferred)

½ cup sour cream

1½ teaspoons curry powder

1 tablespoon lime juice

Dice, slice, or halve main ingredients so they are of a uniform size, about the size of half a grape. Mix main ingredients in a large bowl. In a separate, smaller bowl, stir dressing ingredients together until well blended. Add dressing to main ingredients and toss gently. Cover and chill until time to serve. For a pretty effect, serve in a bowl lined with crisp lettuce leaves and place extra whole grapes or mandarin oranges in a design on top of the salad.

Serves 10 to 12 as a main dish.

Sweet and Tasty Wild Rice Salad
From the kitchen of Geri Wilimek.

---

4 cups cooked wild rice (page 26)

⅓ cup brown sugar

¼ cup oil

2 teaspoons salt

1 teaspoon pepper

6 hard-cooked eggs, chopped

1 small onion, chopped

½ cup mayonnaise

2 teaspoons prepared mustard

While the rice is still warm, toss with brown sugar, oil, salt, and pepper. Stir in remaining ingredients. Chill before serving.

Serves 4 to 6.

Warm and Nutty Wild Rice Salad
From the kitchen of Nancy Lee-Borden.

1½ cups cooked wild rice (page 26)

1 cup peas, frozen, uncooked

4 green onions, sliced

¼ slivered almonds, toasted

2 stalks celery, thinly sliced

Dressing

2 tablespoons wine vinegar

1 tablespoon soy sauce

1 teaspoon sugar

¼ cup oil

2 teaspoons sesame oil (optional)

Warm the wild rice. Toss all ingredients together; toss in dressing. Best if served warm.

Serves 4.

 ## Tarragon and Chicken Wild Rice Salad
From the kitchen of Lee Lehmann.

The distinctive flavor in this recipe is tarragon. I use two tablespoons, but you might like to use less to start, and add to taste.

⅔ cup mayonnaise

⅓ cup milk

2 tablespoons lemon juice

1–2 tablespoons tarragon

3 cups cooked chicken, cubed

3 cups cooked wild rice (page 26)

1 8-ounce can sliced water chestnuts, drained

½ teaspoon salt

¼ teaspoon cracked pepper

1½–2 cups seedless grapes (green or red), cut in half

1 cup salted cashews

Blend mayonnaise, milk, lemon juice, and tarragon, and set aside. In a large bowl, combine chicken, wild rice, water chestnuts, salt, and pepper. Stir in mayonnaise mixture and chill. Just before serving, stir in grapes and cashews.

Serves 8 (1 cup servings).

 ## Wild Rice Garlic Chicken Salad
From the kitchen of Carol Jessen-Klixbull.

---

1 boneless, skinless chicken breast*

1 tablespoon flour

1 tablespoon butter

2 cups cooked wild rice (page 26)

¾ cup red grapes

¼ cup red onion, thinly sliced

½ cup small fresh mushrooms, quartered

1 tart apple, diced into quarter-inch pieces

¼ cup garlic ranch dressing

4–6 lettuce leaves

⅓ lb. bacon, crisply fried and crumbled
1 ripe avocado, sliced into wedges for garnishing

Wash chicken breast and pat dry with paper towel. Dredge in flour and fry in butter for 5 to 7 minutes on each side. When chicken is golden brown and done on the inside, remove from heat and slice diagonally into strips (about ¼-inch wide and 1½-inch long). Refrigerate until cool. Mix chicken with wild rice, grapes, red onion, mushrooms, apple, and dressing. Serve salad on lettuce leaves and garnish with bacon and avocado wedges.

*Any leftover chicken or turkey can be used in place of the chicken breasts. Water chestnuts may be substituted for the apple. Slivered almonds are another tasty addition to the salad. Hard-cooked egg slices can be used instead of the avocado wedges for garnishing. Serving suggestions: Serve with fresh fruit and a hot French loaf or a sweet muffin.

Serves 4 to 6.

 # Wild Rice Salad with Hard-Cooked Eggs
From the kitchen of Peggy Nohner.

Mike and Claudia Verdun shared this recipe with us at a neighborhood potluck. It soon became our favorite dish to share at potlucks.

4 cups cooked wild rice (page 26)
¼ cup cooking oil

2 teaspoons salt
1 teaspoon pepper
6 hard-cooked eggs, sliced
1 small onion
1 cup mayonnaise
2 teaspoons mustard
1 cup green peas, uncooked

Cook the rice. While it is still warm, add remaining ingredients and toss together. Chill before serving.

Serves 6 to 8.

Wild Rice and Bean Salad
From the kitchen of Allen Oster.

3 cups cooked wild rice (page 26)
1 can pinto beans, drained
1 can black beans, drained
1 can green chiles, chopped
½ cup chopped onion
½ cup chopped celery
Italian salad dressing to moisten thoroughly

Combine the ingredients; serve chilled.

Serves 6 to 8.

Soups

WILD RICE FAST FOOD SOUP
Just before serving, add cooked wild rice (page 26) to your favorite soup recipe; heat to a simmer.

 ## Karen's Overnight Cream of Wild Rice Soup
From the kitchen of Karen Skoog.

Letting this sit in the fridge overnight brings out the flavors.

- 2 tablespoons butter
- 1 tablespoon minced onion
- ¼ cup flour
- 4 cups chicken broth
- 2 cups cooked wild rice (page 26)
- ½ teaspoon salt
- 1 cup half and half
- ½ cup tiny pieces of ham (optional)
- ½ cup thinly diced carrots
- ½ cup celery, finely diced
- ½ cup slivered almonds

Sauté onion in butter until tender. Blend in flour and gradually add the broth. Cook, stirring constantly, until thickens slightly. Stir in rice and salt; simmer 5 minutes. Blend in half and half, add ham, carrots, celery, and almonds. Bring to a low simmer and cook 5 minutes. Refrigerate overnight and use the next day.

Serves 6 to 8.

Cream of Wild Rice Soup with Bacon
From the kitchen of Pamela Hanson.

¼ pound bacon
1 large rib celery, sliced
½ large onion, chopped
1 cup cooked wild rice (page 26)
2 cans cream of mushroom soup
1 10¾-ounce can chicken broth
1¼ cans milk (use broth can to measure)
1 4-ounce can mushrooms, or more
dash pepper
⅛ teaspoon Beaumonde

Fry bacon until crisp. Sauté celery and onion in bacon fat; drain. Combine all ingredients and simmer about 20 minutes.

Serves 6 to 8.

Cream of Potato and Wild Rice Soup
From the kitchen of Gourmet House, Clearbrook, Minnesota.

---

1 tablespoon instant minced onion
1 cup water

1 10¾-ounce can cream of potato soup
1 cup half and half
1 cup American cheese, shredded
1 cup cooked wild rice (page 26)
3 slices cooked and crumbled bacon

Put onion and water in a 2- to 3-quart heavy sauce pan. Boil 3 minutes, covered. Stir in soup and blend until smooth. Add the half and half, cheese, and wild rice. Simmer, cooking over low heat until cheese is melted and soup warm. Divide into warmed soup bowls and garnish with crumbled bacon.

Serves 4.

Cream of Wild Rice Soup with Sherry

From the kitchen of Peggy Nohner.

6 tablespoons butter
1 tablespoon minced onion
½ cup flour
3 cups chicken broth
2 cups cooked wild rice (page 26)
½ teaspoon salt
1 cup half and half
2 tablespoons dry sherry or dry white wine
Snipped parsley or chives

Melt butter in sauce pan; sauté onion until tender. Blend in flour; gradually stir in chicken broth. Cook, stirring constantly, until mixture comes to a boil. Continue to boil and stir for 1 minute. Stir in rice and salt; simmer about 5 minutes. Blend in cream and sherry or wine. Heat to serving temperature. Garnish with parsley or chives.

Serves 6.

Variation:
Creamed Wild Rice Soup with Ham

With wild rice and salt, stir in ⅓ cup minced ham, ⅓ cup finely shredded carrot, and 3 tablespoons lightly toasted slivered almonds.

 # Quick Wild Rice and Black Bean Soup
From the kitchen of the author.

---

1 can black beans
1–2 cans canned chicken broth
1 cup cooked wild rice (page 26)

Drain and rinse the black beans. Add to broth and rice in a pan or microwave bowl; heat to a simmer. Serve hot. If desired, sprinkle with shredded (not grated) parmesan cheese.

Serves 2 to 3.

Wild Rice Broth Soup
From the kitchen of Peggy Nohner.

Joan Forbes gave me this recipe when I was looking for an addition to our Thanksgiving dinner. It's been served nearly every Thanksgiving since!

1 pound bacon
3 tablespoons bacon drippings
¾ cup celery, chopped
1 cup onion, chopped
⅓ cup green pepper, chopped
1½ cups cooked wild rice (page 26)
4 cups chicken broth (2-14.5 ounce cans)
¼ cup canned mushrooms
3 10¾-ounce cans mushroom soup

Fry bacon until crisp. Remove strips from pan and sauté celery, onion, and green pepper in 3 tablespoons of the drippings. When vegetables are transparent put in a large kettle with remaining ingredients. Simmer on low heat for one hour or more.

Serves 8.

Sherried Wild Rice Soup

From the kitchen of MacDougall's California Wild Rice, Marysville, California.

Excellent on a chilly evening.

4 tablespoons unsalted butter
1 onion, diced
1 carrot, diced or shredded
2 ribs celery, diced
12 cups homemade chicken stock
2 cups cooked wild rice (page 26)
¾ cup sherry
½ cup minced parsley or cilantro
¼ teaspoon thyme
2 cups mushrooms, quartered

Melt half the butter in large casserole. Add onion, carrot, and celery, and sauté until vegetables become limp and onion turns sweet, stirring occasionally. Add chicken stock, wild rice, sherry, parsley or cilantro, and thyme. Simmer, partially covered for 45 minutes. Meanwhile, melt butter in sauté pan and sauté mushrooms in batches over medium high heat. As they become browned, add to the soup. Continue simmering for 30 minutes. Soup improves in flavor if allowed to stand 1 to 2 hours before serving.

Serves 12 as a first course, 8 as a main dish.

Wenabozhoo: The Origins and Discovery of Wild Rice

L ife was easy for Wenabozhoo. His indulgent grandmother, with whom he lived, demanded no work of him, and in consequence he passed through his early boyhood days without exhibiting any particular interest in those things that must be learned and thoroughly understood by people who depend largely upon self for the necessaries of life.

At last, the grandmother awoke to the fact that her grandson lacked the initiative so essential to meet the requirements of their race, and convinced that her solicitous care was responsible, the aging woman urged the indifferent youth to prepare himself with a training that would fit *him to endure such hardships as hunger, thirst, and cold. She told him that experiences of this kind would make him resourceful and teach him how to care for himself and those who might be dependent upon him. Probably somewhat irked by these plain words, Wenabozhoo later said good-bye to his grandmother, who for many years had provided him with food and shelter.*

Equipped with only a bow and some arrows, he started on a long journey through the forest. For meat, he had to depend upon the flesh of small animals. Not because there was a scarcity of animals, for they abounded in the woods, but because of his unskilled use of the bow, his kills were few. Therefore, he had to subsist on seeds, roots, and tubers. Without knowing the plants that could furnish nourishing food, he naturally made mistakes.

One day when thoroughly exhausted from want of food he heard a voice saying, "Sometimes they eat us." He heard this voice several times and finally asked, "To whom are you talking?" A small bush replied that it had spoken. As no part of the bush above the ground seemed edible, Wenabozhoo thought that the roots might be good to eat. He uncovered the roots, tasted them, and liked the flavor of them very much. Being hungry, he ate many of them and suffered from overeating. For several days he was unable to travel, and when he attempted to do so he found himself as hungry as before and quite weak. As he passed along seeking food, many plants spoke to him. Wenabozhoo gave no heed to their entreaties until he was attracted by the beauty of a graceful grass growing in a small lake basking in the sunshine of the open woodland. Some of these plants beck-

oned to him and said, "Sometimes they eat us." He was quite hungry now, and observing that the upper part of the plants was loaded with long seeds, he soon gathered some of them. Removing the hulls, he ate the kernels and found the taste of them so pleasing and their effect upon his hunger so gratifying that he exclaimed, "Oh, you are indeed good! What are you called?" The plants replied, "We are called manomin."

This version of the Ojibwe discovery story of wild rice was recounted in 1940 by Charles E. Chambliss, President of the Washington Academy of Sciences, in *The Botany and History of Zizanie Aquatica L. (Wild Rice)*. According to his notes, he borrowed the story from Melvin Gilmore, as told in *Prairie Smoke*, 1929.

In *Wild Rice: America's First Grain*, 1943, Robert R. Reed tells this story:

Long ago a young Chippewa youth, obeying the custom among young men of his nation, went away into the forest where he would be cast upon his own resources for food and shelter. He wandered in the wilderness for many days, subsisting on vegetable foods he could find or animals he could shoot or snare.

But after a while food became so scarce that he had to eat some unfamiliar roots which made him very sick. After that, he was very careful what he ate, and sometimes he became quite hungry rather than eat strange fruit and roots. One day he came to a lake in which was growing a strange feathery grass which waved in the wind. He had never seen this grain before, so he did not know that it was good for food. But he was attracted by the beauty of the plants, and as the lake was too muddy and deep for him to wade into the water, he fashioned a canoe of birch-bark and paddled out upon the lake and gathered some of the green stalks to take back to his tribe.

While the seeds were still green, the women planted them in another lake near their wigwams so that this grain would grow there and they could enjoy seeing its beauty.

When the rice which the women had planted had grown to maturity, a very wise old Indian, who traveled a great deal, came to their settlement, and when he saw the wild rice growing he cried, "Mahnomen! Mahnomen!" And he told the Chippewas that Mahnomen or wild rice was good to eat. And they have used it ever since.

As with so many of the stories of the Ojibwe and other American Indian tribes, these retellings come to us through non-Indian sources. Ojibwe scholar Earl Nyholm has mixed feelings about the publication of Indian stories and legends. The written English word allows the stories to be preserved in some form but, at the same time, stories told out of the context of Indian life relay only the plot of the stories and do not convey their additional meanings.[1]

Traditionally, such stories were told for a number of reasons. They affirmed cultural beliefs, they instructed the children, they perpetuated values, and they entertained. Some versions of the stories were told only at certain times. For instance, the maple syrup discovery stories were told only during maple sugaring time and only in the sugar bush. To tell them at other times and places would be rude, like talking about someone who was not present.

The stories were also told to honor and to communicate with the spirits, but when the stories are told in English, said Nyholm, the spirits cannot understand them. The old people, he said, tell us that the spirits only speak and understand the Ojibwe tongue.

It is perhaps difficult for us to understand the implications of the role of wild rice in Ojibwe life. Nyholm spoke of the difference today between a traditional Indian approach to the earth and our contemporary view. For example, he said, the old people tell us that the man who hunts a deer and is hungry for food is seen as a bit pathetic and in need of help. Therefore, the deer allows itself to be killed, out of compassion for the poor man.

In this same way, *manoomin* is made available by the spirits. That it grows in the "spirited environment of water" further confirms its relation to the spirit world. The old people recognized their dependence on the spirits, and on the creatures and elements of the earth. One way they express their thanks for the generosity of both is through the telling of legends and stories.[2]

There are many versions of *manoomin* discovery stories, but all relay one common theme, says Thomas Vennum in *Wild Rice and the Ojibwe People*: ". . . the Wenabozhoo legends make it clear that wild rice was, above all, a food especially intended for the Indian people." Further, says Vennum, the ancient Ojibwe belief says that *manoomin* was seeded in the lakes by the supernatural beings. He repeats a story told by Bill Johnson, a Nett Lake Ojibwe, in 1947 to Jenks in *The Wild Rice Gatherers of the Upper Lakes* (1900), which the narrator "had learned from his grandfather, that wild rice was created for the *anishinaabeg* (original people): 'Man has never planted the rice; it had been put in [Nett Lake] and other lakes and rivers, when the land was formed for the Indians. Also, one cannot sow the rice; humans can't do that. Sometimes there is no rice, but when the *manidoog* (spirits) want it, it grows again.'"[3]

In addition to storytelling, the gift of *manoomin* was acknowledged through ceremony. A feast that featured the first harvest of rice was held at the ricing camp, and *manoomin* was served at other ceremonies and family feasts.[4] But it was also used as an everyday food and was eaten all year round, by itself or in stews, soups, and other dishes, not just at harvest or through the winter.

Manoomin was not only an everyday food but an everyday medicine, says Vennum, in a way that is "distinct from Ojibway beliefs and practices that accord it more special powers." Cooked rice was made into gruels and juices and combined with other ingredients, such as herbs, and were used as milk substitutes, poultices, and salves. These everyday uses, says Vennum, differ from uses of wild rice that are spiritually based, such as its use during pregnancy and puberty rites.[5]

Wild rice continues today to be an integral part of Indian life, and provides a continuity with the past, said Nyholm. People return to the Indian reservations for the wild rice harvest, as for centuries they returned to their wild rice camps. As with maple sugaring, it is a tradition that does not have to be reclaimed, said Nyholm, because it has never been lost.

Before *manoomin* was discovered by Wenabozhoo, before there were lakes and rivers in the western Great Lakes area, before there were Great Lakes, there was ice. "A Study of Possible Prehistoric Wild Rice Gathering on Lake of the Woods, Ontario," tells of the changes that followed the recession of the glaciers: about nine thousand years ago, the land around the western Great Lakes

The Turtle River rice beds, in northern Minnesota, have been riced for as long as stories have been told. This rice, in August 1998, is almost ready for harvest. Photographer: Vivienne Morgan. Canoeist: Dave Carlson.

area was cool and moist; around seven thousand years ago, it was warmer and drier; about three thousand years ago, it became cooler and wetter; the climate has changed little since then.[6]

With the change to a cool, moist climate came the generation of bogs and muskegs. Although grass *(Gramineae)* pollens from as long ago as nine thousand years have been identified, a majority of wild rice pollen does not appear until three thousand years ago, during what geologists call the Laurel or Middle Woodland period.[7]

During that time, several major events occurred in addition to the apparent proliferation of wild rice: there was a population explosion; ceramics were first being used; and the Laurel People were constructing and using burial mounds.[8]

There is evidence of the beginning of wild rice use by humans in the correlation between the location of villages and wild rice lakes in the Ontario Lake of the Woods area. The correlation, however, does not prove that the Laurel People of the period were actually utilizing the rice. They may have lived there because the rice attracted waterfowl, or for other reasons.[9]

There have been findings, however, on an excavation in St. Louis County, Minnesota, in the vicinity of the Lake Superior city of Duluth, of pottery sherds that indicate wild rice processing.[10] Excavations in Michigan uncovered ricing pits, used to separate parched wild rice from its hulls, and charred rice kernels have been found that date to about the same period as the St. Louis County and Lake of the Woods sites, approximately three thousand years ago, coincident with the Laurel period.[11]

Such findings, of course, are subject to adjustment based on new archaeological evidence and techniques. Some archaeologists believe that is was the emergence and proliferation of wild rice itself, as an abundant and nutritious food source, that accounts for the sudden population growth among the Laurel People, and thereby also accounts for the emergence of ceramic technology and burial mound practices.[12]

Wenabozhoo, I think, would agree.

❊ Entrees and Casseroles ❊

Entrees

Shrimp or Chicken Wild Rice Sauté   79
Spinach and Wild Rice Sauté   79
Quick Cheese, Spinach, and Wild Rice   80
Quick Black Bean and Wild Rice Stew   81
Lentil and Wild Rice Loaf   81
Cashew and Wild Rice Patties   82
Green Peppers with Wild Rice Stuffing   83
Turkey Wild Rice Loaf with Ginger Cranberry Compote   84
Morel and Chicken Wild Rice Risotto   85
Chicken and Wild Rice Bake   86
Henry Wellington's Blackened Chicken Jambalaya with Wild Rice   87
Wild Rice Chicken Escallops with Fruited Wild Rice Stuffing   88
Ham and Wild Rice Tart   89
Wild Rice Meat Loaf   90
Hamburger Wild Rice Steaks with Bleu Cheese and Mushrooms   91
Wild Rice Preserves Garlic   92
Pork with Apple and Wild Rice   92
Pork Chops with Wild Rice and Cranberry Walnut Stuffing   93
Wild Rice Chili   94
Poached Fillet of Sole with Wild Rice, Cilantro, and Lime   94

Casseroles

Entrees

Shrimp or Chicken Wild Rice Sauté
From the kitchen of Marsh Muirhead.

Cook up some wild rice in the usual manner, a cup or two of cooked rice per serving for the hearty eaters I know. Pull it off the burner *just* as it's about done. Simultaneously, poach, just to done, either strips of chicken breast or jumbo shrimp or cook the meat in a wok or a large sauté pan. Give the meat some zip—your choice of spices. I like to add lots of garlic and pepper, or hot sauce, or butter and Cajun seasoning. Turn up the heat in the pan so the meat gets browned and the butter, if added, is almost going to burn. Then, toss in the rice and mix it all up like mad. The remaining moisture in the rice should boil off and the rice will sear or fry here and there.

Spinach and Wild Rice Sauté
From the kitchen of Nancy R. Kapp.

½ cup butter
¼ cup chopped fresh chives
¼ cup chopped fresh parsley
2 cups chopped fresh spinach
½ cup mild, red-skinned radishes, thinly sliced

4 cups cooked wild rice (page 26)
1–1½ teaspoons salt

In large skillet, melt butter and sauté chives, parsley, and spinach until they become limp. Stir in radish slices and wild rice. Reduce heat and cook until warm. Stir in salt.

Serves 4 to 6.

 ## Quick Cheese, Spinach, and Wild Rice
From the kitchen of MacDougall's California Wild Rice, Marysville, California.

Oil
1 yellow or red onion, chopped
2 cloves garlic, minced
1½ cups cooked wild rice (page 26)
1 bunch spinach, washed and chopped
⅓ cup grated cheese
Soy sauce to taste
Optional: Sautéed mushrooms

In a large frying pan, sauté the onions and garlic until onions are transparent. Stir in the wild rice. Add chopped spinach and stir. Cover pan and cook until spinach is wilted. Add grated cheese and cook additional 5 minutes. Season with soy sauce to taste. Serve with sautéed mushrooms, if desired.

Serves 4.

QUICK BLACK BEAN AND WILD RICE STEW
Rinse 1 can of black beans and mix in saucepan or microwave dish with 1 cup cooked wild rice. Season to taste (cumin is nice). Heat and serve.

 ## Lentil and Wild Rice Loaf
From the kitchen of Andrew and Debbie Warne-Jacobsen.

Leftovers from this loaf make excellent sandwiches.

1½ cups water
1½ tablespoons liquid aminos or soy sauce, divided
¾ cup dry brown lentils
1 cup cooked wild rice (page 26)
½ cup oat bran
½ cup minced celery
½ cup chopped walnuts
2 cloves minced garlic
2 teaspoons onion powder
½ teaspoon curry
½ teaspoon dill
½ teaspoon fennel
½ teaspoon pepper
½ teaspoon sage

Bring water to a boil in a saucepan; add ¾ tablespoon aminos and lentils. Reduce heat and simmer for 30 minutes or until tender. Do not drain.

In a bowl, stir together the lentils and aminos mixture with the remaining ingredients, including remaining ¾ tablespoon aminos. Mix well, until the lentils and rice have fused (the lentils will break down). Place in a greased or nonstick loaf pan and shape into an oval. Brush with remaining aminos. Bake at 375°F for 45 to 60 minutes or until crisp on the outside. Remove from oven and let stand for 10 minutes. Slice or wedge and serve.

Serves 4 to 6.

 ## Cashew and Wild Rice Patties
From the kitchen of the author.

---

1 cup cooked wild rice (page 26)
¼ cup chopped nuts (such as cashews, almonds, pecans, or walnuts)
2 tablespoons flour
1 egg or 2 egg whites
Salt and pepper to taste (omit salt if nuts are salted)

Mix ingredients together. Lightly grease a frying pan and heat to medium high. With a spoon, place the mixture in the pan in 3 or 4 dollops and shape into patties. The mixture will be loose at first, but will firm up with cooking. Cook about 3 minutes on each side. Serve as an entree or a side dish. To serve as an appetizer, make the patties smaller.

Makes 3 entrees or a dozen appetizer patties.

Green Peppers with Wild Rice Stuffing
From the kitchen of Allen Oster.

This stuffing may also be used for cabbage rolls.

6 green peppers
½ pound hamburger
½ pound pork sausage
2 tablespoons chopped shallots
1½ cups cooked wild rice
1 teaspoon salt
⅛ teaspoon garlic
1 can finely chopped water chestnuts
15-ounce can tomato sauce
15-ounce can crushed tomatoes

Clean peppers and boil for 5 minutes. Brown hamburger, sausage, and shallots; add remaining ingredients except tomato sauce and crushed tomatoes. Fill peppers with mixture. Pour tomato sauce and crushed tomatoes over peppers. Cover and bake at 350°F for 45 minutes. Uncover and bake 15 minutes longer.

Serves 4 to 6.

Turkey Wild Rice Loaf with Ginger Cranberry Compote

From the kitchen of Mary Clemenson.

1 pound ground turkey breast

¼ cup chopped onion

¾ cup well-drained cooked wild rice (page 26)

1 tablespoon Worcestershire sauce

¼ teaspoon salt

Freshly ground black pepper to taste

1 teaspoon dried parsley

1 teaspoon dried sage

1 egg white

Combine all the above ingredients, mixing well. Turn into greased 8½x4½-inch loaf pan. Bake at 350°F for 30 minutes or until firm.

Ginger Cranberry Compote

12 ounces fresh or frozen cranberries, picked over and rinsed

¾ cup water

¼ cup brown sugar

¼ cup granulated sugar

2 whole cloves

⅛ teaspoon cayenne pepper or as desired

⅛ teaspoon allspice

1 teaspoon ground ginger

¼ cup raisins

1 medium firm, ripe Bartlett pear, unpeeled and finely diced

Combine cranberries, water, sugars, and spices in heavy saucepan. Bring to a boil uncovered over high heat, stirring frequently. When mixture boils and berries begin to pop, reduce heat to medium. Cook 8 to 10 minutes longer, until all berries have popped and mixture has begun to thicken. Add raisins and diced pear; cook about 2 minutes longer until the pear pieces are soft yet retain their shape. Serve warm with wild rice turkey loaf.

Serves 6.

Morel and Chicken Wild Rice Risotto
From the kitchen of Michael and Vivienne Morgan.

The trick is to precook the wild rice and mix it with arborio rice. If you can't find morels (look during mid- to late May, after a wet spell, in old popple stands), try substituting portobellos.

⅓ cup uncooked wild rice

1 shallot or small onion

2 cloves garlic

¼ pound fresh morels (about 8 largish ones)

1–2 tablespoons olive oil

1 cup arborio rice

1 chicken breast, boned and cut into 1-inch chunks

3 cups chicken stock
¼ cup parsley

Cook the wild rice until nearly done. It won't cook much more in the risotto. Drain excess water. Chop fine the shallot, garlic, and one or two of the smaller morels. Sauté this mixture in the olive oil for 3 to 4 minutes over medium-high heat. Add arborio rice and cooked wild rice and sauté for a few more minutes. Add chicken to the pan and cook until chicken turns white. Keeping heat on medium or a little higher, start adding the stock, ½ cup at a time. Add, stir, let bubble until the stock is absorbed, repeat. Watch the risotto (rice and broth mixture) carefully so it doesn't burn. Lower the heat if the stock seems to be cooking away too quickly. Adding the stock in small amounts should take 20 to 30 minutes. Just before the risotto is done—it will still be al dente, and you will have ¼ to ½ of stock left to add—add the remaining morels, parsley, and a little more stock if necessary, and stir gently. Cook a minute or so more. Don't let the morels cook too long or they will wither away to nothing. Remove from heat. Add salt and pepper if you feel the need.

Serves 4 as a starter, 2 if you're hungry.

 ## Chicken and Wild Rice Bake
From the kitchen of Nancy R. Kapp.

1 package Uncle Ben's Long Grain and Wild Rice
½ cup uncooked wild rice

1 can cream of onion soup
1 soup can of water
6 split chicken breasts
1 can cream of chicken soup

Place rice in 9x13-inch baking dish. Put package of herbs from Uncle Ben's over rice. Pour onion soup and water over mixture. Place chicken on top of mixture. Put chicken soup over all. Bake at 350°F for 2 hours.

Serves 4 to 6.

 ## Henry Wellington's Blackened Chicken Jambalaya with Wild Rice

From the kitchen of Henry Wellington, a Restaurant, Red Wing, Minnesota.

For each serving:
1 boneless, skinned chicken breast
Cajun blackening spices (Paul Prudhomme's, etc.)
1 cup Henry Wellington's Wild Rice (page 127)
3 ounces cooked vegetables (broccoli, cauliflower, mushroom, onion, or favorite mix)
2 ounces tomato juice
½ teaspoon gumbo file

Coat chicken breast with blackening spices, and blacken: heat a heavy cast-iron fry pan as hot as possible on the stove top, and lay the coated chicken breast on it; turn once when first side is blackened and blacken the other side. (Note: Blackening produces a lot of smoke. Proper ventilation is required.) Slice blackened chicken into thin strips. Warm rice and vegetables in microwave, and combine with chicken in frying pan. Add tomato juice and gumbo file and mix well. Stir over medium heat until all is hot and well mixed. Shrimp may be substituted for the chicken.

Wild Rice Chicken Escallops with Fruited Wild Rice Stuffing

From the kitchen of Gourmet House, Clearwater, Minnesota.

1¾ cups cooked wild rice (page 26)
½ cup dried apricots, chopped
2 tablespoons raisins
¼ cup butter, softened
Salt and pepper to taste
1 egg white
¼ cup fresh bread crumbs
¼ cup nuts, chopped (toasted optional)
5 chicken breasts, 3 ounces each, pounded thin
¼ cup fresh, sliced mushrooms
¼ cup minced shallots
1 teaspoon minced thyme
1 cup dry white wine

Mix wild rice, apricots, raisins, half the butter, salt, pepper, egg white, bread crumbs, and nuts. Spread approximately ½ cup mixture on each chicken breast, roll, and tie with string; set aside. Sauté mushrooms and shallots in remaining butter 5 minutes. Season with thyme, salt, and pepper. Remove mushroom mixture from pan; set aside. Flour rolled chicken breasts; brown in same pan. Add wine and mushroom mixture; cover and braise 15 minutes over low heat. Slice and serve with mushrooms and shallots.

Serves 4 to 6.

 ## Ham and Wild Rice Tart
From the kitchen of Carolyn Reiersgaard.

I usually make this around holidays because that's when I have leftovers. It's a pretty tart to serve with a salad.

Filling
1 cup cubed cooked ham
½ cup cooked wild rice (page 26), drained
⅓ cup finely chopped red bell pepper
¼ cup thinly sliced green onion tops
½ pound sliced fresh mushrooms
    or 1 4.5 ounce jar, drained
2 cups (8 ounces) shredded low-fat Swiss cheese

Custard

3 eggs
1 cup Sour Lean
1 tablespoon Dijon mustard
$\frac{1}{2}$ teaspoon salt
$\frac{1}{8}$ teaspoon pepper

Garnish

Pecan halves

Make a 9-inch pie crust. Bake at 425°F for 10 minutes or so. Remove from oven and reduce heat to 400°F. Toss filling items together and in crust. Blend custard ingredients and pour over filling. Garnish with pecans and bake for 30 minutes or until custard is set.

Serves 6 to 8.

Wild Rice Meat Loaf
From the kitchen of Nancy R. Kapp.

---

1 pound ground beef
3 eggs, beaten
2 cups cooked wild rice (page 26)
2 stalks celery, chopped
$\frac{3}{4}$ cups fresh mushrooms, chopped
1 teaspoon salt
$\frac{1}{4}$ teaspoon pepper

Combine all ingredients and mix well. Put into a 9x5x3-inch loaf pan. Bake at 350°F for 1 hour. Let cool in pan for 10 minutes. Drain excess juices and turn loaf out onto serving platter. Slice and top with cheese sauce.

Cheese Sauce
2 tablespoons butter
2 tablespoons flour
1 cup milk
1 cup grated cheddar cheese

Melt butter over low heat and stir in flour, blending well. Slowly stir in milk, cooking and stirring constantly. Cook until smooth and thickened. Add cheese and stir until cheese is melted.

Serves 4 to 6.

 ## Hamburger Wild Rice Steaks with Bleu Cheese and Mushrooms
From the kitchen of Barb and Myron Wagner.

Soooo tasty . . . serve as you would steaks—without buns.

1½ cups cooked wild rice (page 26)
1 egg
2 teaspoons Worcestershire sauce
1 teaspoon salt
½ teaspoon fresh ground pepper
1½ pounds lean hamburger

2 cups fresh mushrooms, sliced
2 tablespoons butter
1 cup crumbled blue cheese

Combine first five ingredients in a large bowl. Add the hamburger, mix together well, and shape 4 to 6 patties. While patties are cooking, sauté the mushrooms in butter. Just before the patties are done, sprinkle with the crumbled blue cheese and allow it to melt slightly. Before serving, spoon mushrooms over the melted cheese. Voilà!

Serves 4 to 6.

WILD RICE PRESERVES GARLIC
From the kitchen of Barb and Myron Wagner.
Whole heads of garlic stored in a container with uncooked wild rice will stay fresh for months.

 ## Pork with Apple and Wild Rice
From the kitchen of Nancy R. Kapp.

4 pork chops
Oil for frying
1 cup uncooked wild rice
1 large onion sliced into rings
2½ cups chicken broth
2 large, red cooking apples

Brown pork chops on both sides in an electric skillet at 375°F, using as little oil as possible. Remove chops and sprinkle rice into pan. Arrange pork chops and onion rings over rice. Pour chicken broth over all. Bring to a boil and lower heat to maintain a slow simmer, about 200°F for an hour. Core and slice the apples, place over top of the pork chops, and simmer 15 minutes, or until apples, rice, and chops are tender.

Serves 4.

Pork Chops with Wild Rice and Cranberry Walnut Stuffing

From the kitchen of MacDougall's California Wild Rice, Marysville, California.

1 red or yellow onion, chopped

2 cloves garlic, minced

Olive oil for sautéing

½ cup scallions (green or white parts)

¼ cup parsley

1 tablespoon thyme, dried or fresh

2 cups cooked wild rice (page 26)

1½ cups cooked whole cranberries

¼ cup finely chopped walnuts

4 1½-inch-thick pork chops, browned in 1 tablespoon olive oil

In large skillet, sauté yellow onion and garlic in olive oil until limp. Add scallions, parsley, and thyme. Stir and continue cooking for 2 minutes.

Add wild rice, cranberries, and walnuts. Stir to combine well. Add salt and pepper to taste. In medium casserole with cover, spread ½ rice mixture. Place browned pork chops on top of rice mixture, and top with remaining mixture. Bake in 350°F oven for 25 minutes.

Serves 4.

WILD RICE CHILI
Ten minutes before serving chili, add 1 cup of cooked wild rice (page 26) for each four cups of chili.

 ## Poached Fillet of Sole with Wild Rice, Cilantro, and Lime
From the kitchen of MacDougall's California Wild Rice, Marysville, California.

4 ¼-inch-thick sole fillets
1 cup cooked wild rice (page 26)
½ cup cilantro
¼ cup grated carrot
Salt and pepper to taste
¾ cup white wine
4 tablespoons butter
3 limes, halved

Wash and pat fillets dry. Combine wild rice, cilantro, and carrot. Add salt and pepper to taste. Lay fillet on work surface. Layer rice mixture over entire fillet ½ inch thick. Roll fillets end to end jelly roll fashion. Repeat with remaining fillets. Place fillets in skillet with lid. Add white wine and enough water to barely cover fillets. Cover and poach gently (do not bring to a boil) 5 to 10 minutes, being careful to not overcook. Remove fillets from liquid carefully with a slotted spoon. Drain on paper towels and cover with foil to keep warm. Bring liquid to a rapid boil and reduce to ½ cup. Add butter and whisk to incorporate. Squeeze halved limes into sauce. Taste after each addition. Sauce should be left tart, but not overpowering. Carefully transfer fish and rice to serving plates. Spoon sauce over fillets and serve immediately.

Serves 4.

Casseroles

In Minnesota, it would not be a picnic, holiday dinner, or family reunion without a wild rice "hot dish."

 ## Tomato and Olives Wild Rice Casserole
From the kitchen of Greg and Paulette Giese.

Nice as a side dish. A favorite at Christmas and Thanksgiving.

1 cup uncooked wild rice
3 cups water
   or 3 cups cooked wild rice (page 26)
½ cup chopped onion
1 cup sliced mushrooms
½ cup butter
1 cup canned tomatoes
1 cup chopped ripe black olives
1 cup grated Cheddar cheese
1 cup hot water

Cook rice until tender, about 35 to 45 minutes. Sauté onions and mushrooms in butter. Combine all ingredients in ungreased casserole, saving out a little cheese to sprinkle on top. Stir in 1 cup hot water last, to keep dish moist. Sprinkle with reserved cheese. Cover and bake for 45 minutes at 350°F.

Serves 6 to 8.

Favorite Hot Wild Rice Dish
From the kitchen of Debbie Drinkard Grovum.

1 cup uncooked wild rice
$^{1}/_{2}$ cup chopped onion
$^{1}/_{2}$ cup chopped celery
8 ounces fresh, sliced mushrooms
$^{1}/_{2}$ cup slivered almonds
2 tablespoons butter
3 cups chicken or vegetable stock

Sauté wild rice, onion, celery, mushrooms, and almonds in butter for 30 minutes. Combine with stock and bake uncovered in a casserole dish at 350°F for 1$^{1}/_{2}$ to 2 hours, until rice is tender and moisture is absorbed.

Serves 6.

Surprise Wild Rice
From the kitchen of Marion Jacobsen.

This recipe can also be cooked in a frying pan on the stovetop.

$^{1}/_{2}$ cup onions, diced
$^{1}/_{2}$ cup celery, chopped
$^{1}/_{2}$ cup fresh mushrooms
1–3 tablespoons butter or oil

3 cups cooked wild rice (page 26)
1 cup chicken broth
1 teaspoon garlic powder
1/2 teaspoon ginger powder
1/2 cup dried cranberries
1/2 cup toasted slivered almonds

Sauté onion, celery, and mushrooms in butter or oil. Mix all ingredients together in a bowl, then place in a greased casserole dish. Bake at 350°F for 30 minutes.

Serves 6 to 8.

 ## Chicken Wild Rice Casserole with White Sauce
From the kitchen of Peggy Nohner.

1/3 cup onion, chopped
1/3 cup green pepper, chopped
2 tablespoons butter
3 tablespoons flour
1 1/4 cup chicken broth
1 1/4 cup milk
1 cup canned sliced mushrooms
2 cups cooked chicken, cubed
1/2 teaspoon salt
1/4 teaspoon pepper

⅛ teaspoon garlic powder
4½ cups cooked wild rice (page 26)
⅓ cup slivered almonds, toasted

Sauté onion and green pepper in butter until tender. Stir in flour. Gradually add broth and stir until well blended. Add milk (this makes the white sauce). Cook and stir until mixture starts to thicken. Mix in remaining ingredients except almonds. Place mixture in 9x13-inch pan or a casserole dish. Sprinkle almonds over the top. Bake at 350°F for 25 to 30 minutes.

Serves 8.

Variations:
Add ½ cup chopped celery and sauté with onion.
Add ½ cup sliced water chestnuts to the mixture.
Add 2 tablespoons sherry to white sauce.

 ## Russell's Good Chicken Hot Dish
From the kitchen of Lisa McLean.

---

1 cup uncooked wild rice
2½ to 3 cups water
 or 3 cups cooked wild rice (page 26)
2 teaspoons salt
4 tablespoons butter

5 tablespoons flour
1 cup chicken broth
1 1/2 cups evaporated milk
2 cups cooked chicken, diced
3/4 cup mushrooms, sliced
1/4 cup pimiento, diced
1/2 cup green pepper, diced
1 cup buttered bread crumbs
    or 1/2 cup sliced almonds
Paprika

Cook wild rice with water and 1 teaspoon of the salt. In a different pan, combine butter, flour, and chicken broth. Simmer over low heat until butter melts. Stir in milk, remaining teaspoon of salt, chicken, mushrooms, pimiento, and green pepper. Add cooked rice. Place in a buttered casserole dish. Cover with bread crumbs or almonds and sprinkle with paprika. Bake at 350°F, uncovered, 30 to 40 minutes.

Serves 8 to 10.

 ## Chicken Wild Rice Casserole with Almonds
From the kitchen of Bea Knodel.

This recipe was contributed by Jackie Decker to a Bemidji State College faculty wives cookbook, circa 1971, and is still a favorite of mine.

1 cup uncooked wild rice

3 cups water

    or 3 cups cooked wild rice (page 26)

6 green onions, chopped

½ green pepper, chopped

1 cup mushrooms, sliced

¼ cup butter

3 tablespoons flour

¼ cup milk

2 cups milk or light cream

¼ pound cheese, grated

2 cups cooked chicken

1 cup slivered almonds

Chopped pimento

Salt and pepper to taste

Cook wild rice for 30 to 60 minutes, until tender. Sauté onion, green pepper, and mushrooms in butter. Add flour and cook briefly. Stir in milk, then light cream, to make a cream sauce, and whisk until smooth. Melt cheese in sauce. Mix all ingredients and season to taste with salt and pepper. Bake in buttered casserole at 350°F for 45 minutes.

Serves 6 or so.

Chicken and Broccoli Wild Rice Casserole
From the kitchen of Nancy R. Kapp.

1 cup cooked wild rice (page 26)
1 pound broccoli cooked and well drained
2 cups shredded Cheddar cheese
3 cups chicken and/or ham
2 cups sliced fresh mushrooms
1 can cream of celery soup
¼ teaspoon dry mustard
¼ teaspoon curry powder
Parmesan cheese
Croutons and butter

Layer rice, broccoli, Cheddar cheese, meat, and mushrooms in a 9x13-inch baking dish. Combine soup, mustard, and curry. Pour over layers. Sprinkle with Parmesan cheese. Top with croutons which have been crumbled and mixed with butter. Bake at 350°F about 30 minutes or until bubbly.

Serves 4 to 6.

Veal and Wild Rice Casserole
From the kitchen of Margaret H. Harlow.

2 pounds veal, cubed
½ cup celery, chopped

½ cup onions, chopped
1 cup mushrooms, sliced
1 cup cooked wild rice (page 26)

Sauté all ingredients except wild rice. Add wild rice. Place mixture in a greased casserole dish and bake at 350°F until vegetables are tender, around 45 minutes. Check occasionally. If ingredients start to get dry stir in some water or chicken broth.

Serves 6 to 8.

 ## Grice and Rice
From the kitchen of Charlie O'Connor.

This came to me from Lyle and Sally Lauber twenty-eight years ago. Substitute a chicken breast if the grouse resists.

1 grouse breast
½ cup onion, diced
½ cup celery, diced
1 cup wild rice, uncooked
½ cup sliced mushrooms
Butter for sautéing
1 teaspoon salt
1 cup sour cream
1 can undiluted mushroom soup

Place grouse breast in large saucepan and cover with at least one quart of water. Simmer for 1 hour and set aside to cool. Sauté the onion and celery in butter. Combine 3 cups of the grouse broth, 1 cup of wild rice, and the sautéed onion and celery. Cover and cook on low for 1 hour. (The rice will split open.) Sauté the ½ cup mushrooms in butter. Flake cooled grouse breast, add to rice mixture along with the sautéed mushrooms and salt. Add sour cream and undiluted chicken soup. Mix well and place in a glass baking dish. Cook uncovered in a 350°F oven for approximately 45 minutes.

Bacon Wild Rice Casserole
From the kitchen of Judy Lykins.

Grandma Bea always made this for Thanksgiving. My sister Sandy or I make it now, and it is truly a family tradition. This recipe is as close as we can get to how Grandma made it.

2 cups uncooked wild rice

6–7 cups water

2 tablespoons chicken bouillon flavoring or 6 bouillon cubes
   or 6 cups cooked wild rice (page 26)

6 slices bacon, fried crisp, drained and crumbled

3 stalks celery, chopped and sautéed in bacon grease

1 can water chestnuts, drained and sliced thin

2 small cans mushrooms, drained

½ cup slivered almonds (optional)

Bake the wild rice, water, and chicken bouillon, covered, for 1 hour at 350°F. Check occasionally and add more water if necessary to keep the rice moist. Stir in remaining ingredients. Continue baking covered 30 minutes. Uncover and bake 5 to 15 minutes more.

Serves 10 to 12.

 ## Ground Beef and Wild Rice Casserole
From the kitchen of Rosemary Given Amble.

This always tastes best when served with roughed grouse during the fall hunting season, or Cornish game hens throughout the rest of the year. I often make a large batch and freeze in small containers for busy days.

2 cups uncooked wild rice

2 quarts water

1 teaspoon salt

   (or 6 cups cooked wild rice [page 26])

¼ cup butter

¼ cup olive oil

1½ pounds lean ground beef

1 cup diced onion

1 cup diced celery

1 small can mushroom stems and pieces

1 can mushroom soup

1 can beef broth

¼ cup soy sauce

Salt and pepper

Wash wild rice. In a large Dutch oven, bring salted water to a boil and add rice. Cover and cook at a strong simmer for 45 minutes. Drain the rice, saving the nutrient-filled liquid. Place drained wild rice back in the Dutch oven. In a heavy skillet melt butter and add olive oil. Brown ground beef with onion and celery. When nicely browned stir in mushroom stems and pieces and mushroom soup. When well heated, slowly add beef broth and soy sauce and bring to a boil. Add to the wild rice in the Dutch oven. Add salt and pepper to taste. Cover and place in 300°F oven for 1 hour. Check periodically and add the reserved wild rice water as necessary to prevent from drying.

Serves 10 to 12.

 ## Sausage and Wild Rice Casserole
From the kitchen of Ginnie Lundsten.

---

1 cup uncooked wild rice
3 cups water
   or 3 cups cooked wild rice (page 26)
1 pound well seasoned bulk sausage
8 ounces fresh mushrooms
   or 2 small cans sliced mushrooms
1 can cream of mushroom soup
1 medium onion, sliced thin

Cook wild rice 35 to 60 minutes (do not let it get mushy). In a frying pan, cook sausage until crumbly. Pour off fat. Add mushrooms and lightly sauté. Stir in soup and cooked wild rice. Spread one half the mixture in a 1½- or 2-quart buttered casserole dish. Layer with onion. Spread remaining onion over mixture. Bake in covered casserole at 350°F for 60 minutes.

Serves 4 to 6.

 ## Pork and Beef Wild Rice Casserole
From the kitchen of Bea Knodel.

One of the lovely things about this recipe is that if the kids don't come in from tobogganing, or your guests are in the middle of a major discussion, it can go on baking for another hour without harm. It came to me from Pat Corrin.

1½ large onions, chopped
1 clove garlic, minced
½ cup butter
1 pound cubed beef round steak
1 pound cubed lean pork
1 cup uncooked wild rice
2½ cups beef stock
    or 2 cups consommé
1 tablespoon soy sauce
    or less if stock is salted
2 cups celery, chopped

½ **pound mushrooms, sliced**
1 **can chopped water chestnuts, drained**
Salt and pepper to taste
½ **cup slivered almonds, toasted**

Sauté onion and garlic in butter until transparent. Add meat and brown. Mix all ingredients except ½ cup of stock and almonds. Place in a casserole dish or 9x13-inch pan. Cover and bake at least 2 hours at 350°F. Check occasionally and add water if necessary to keep moist. Just before serving, stir in the last ½ cup stock and sprinkle with almonds.

Serves 8 or so.

Naturally occurring wild rice marshes. Above: *Zizania palustris*, Turtle River, Minnesota, August 1998. *Vivienne Morgan*

Below: Sora rail trapline through *Zizania aquatica*, Patuxent River, Maryland, 1996. The yellow flowers are bur marigold, *Bidens laevi*s. *Michael Haramis, USGS Patuxent Wildlife Research Center*

zania palustris growing in a DeWit Farms e field in the Sacramento Valley, California, tober 1998. *Susan Carol Hauser*

This long grain wild rice, which grows in natural rice beds in Canada and some areas of Minnesota, is a variety of *Zizania palustris*.

The length of this Minnesota lake rice is typical of most western Great Lakes wild rice, both cultivated and naturally occurring, and cultivated rice grown in California.

Brown wild rice. This processed wild rice is brown in color because more of its bran has been removed during processing. Brown wild rice has a mild flavor and cooks in about 30 to 45 minutes. The amount of bran removed is nutritionally insignificant. Both naturally occurring and cultivated wild rice can be processed this way.

Black wild rice. Processed wild rice that is black has most of its bran layer still intact; it has a distinct flavor and cooks in about 45 to 60 minutes. Both naturally occurring and cultivated wild rice can be processed this way.

Images by Vivienne Morgan

This rice is just starting to cook. Note that most kernels are still closed.

This rice is underdone. Some of the kernels have opened, but most are closed.

This rice is ready to serve. Most of the kernels are split open, and some are "butterflied." It will be tender, yet will still have a chewy texture. It is ideal for serving as a side dish, a main dish, or in casseroles or stuffings.

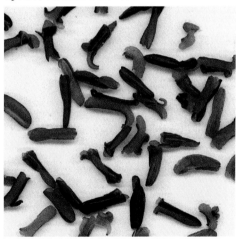

This rice is overdone. Most of the kernels are "butterflied." Most people will find it too soft for use as a side or main dish. It is, however, desirable for use in breads.

Images by Vivienne Morgan

Zizania palustris. Note that the lower male flowers are opening upward along the stem, and that the female flowers, in the green head at the top, are not yet open. Cross-pollination is encouraged by this arrangement of the flowers.
Vivienne Morgan

F   I   V   E

Zizania palustris

The cultivation of wild rice did not begin with the 1950s and '60s development of artificial wild rice paddies. In many versions of the *manoomin* discovery stories, it begins with the first gift of wild rice to Wenabozhoo, as in the story recounted by Robert R. Reed, and relayed in Chapter Four: *While the seeds were still green, the women planted them in another lake near their wigwams so that this grain would grow there and they could enjoy seeing its beauty* (*Wild Rice: America's First Grain*, 1943).

That spiritual sowing of the first rice is, of course, different from intentional propagation. There are differing opinions in the Ojibwe community about the wisdom of intentional planting: it might be considered an affront to the Great Spirit. Nevertheless, many Ojibwe report the seeding of natural rice beds.[1]

Non-native observers also report the early-on tending of wild rice as a crop. D. Wayne Moodie, in his *Aboriginal Resource Use in Canada*, tells us that in 1935 "Sister Inez Hilger . . . observed: 'At the present time on this reservation (Lac du Flambeau, Wisconsin) people scatter rice on lake shores a few days after they have gathered it. . . . They sow the rice so that the Chippewa in the future—maybe relatives—will have wild rice.'" Moodie also reports that a 1935 study of wild rice states that "'long before the Ojibwa had any contact with Europeans, it was usual to wrap a few grains (of wild rice) in clay and throw them into the water to make new plants for the ensuing year.'"[2]

Such practices are still carried out today in lake and river stands. It is common for ricers to donate a coffee can of wild rice seed from their harvest to reseed beds that are in decline,[3] and rice is sometimes harvested from Reservation lakes to use as seed for Reservation rice beds.[4]

The replenishment and maintenance of wild rice stands, and even the development of new stands in natural waters by American Indians, was most likely originally carried out for the perpetuation of wild rice as a food crop. And while European explorers, trappers, and traders often subsisted on the wild rice, and valued it for its nutrition and flavor, apparently by the turn of the twentieth century, the primary interest in propagating it was not as a food for people, but as food to attract ducks and birds for hunting.

In a 1903 article on wild rice published by the United States Bureau of Plant Industry, Edgar Brown says ". . . by far the largest demand for information regarding this plant has come from men or organizations wishing to secure viable seed for planting near shooting grounds to attract wild fowl."[5] This sentiment is reiterated in a 1924 article by Donald Hough: "It (wild rice) has grown into quite an industry, for shooting clubs are anxious to get the rice to plant on their reserves."[6]

The trend persisted at least into the 1940s, as noted in a 1986 article: "Wild rice was originally planted in Idaho 40 years ago by duck hunters who wanted to provide forage for their feathered targets."[7] As with most early efforts, these plantings seem to have taken place in naturally occurring lakes and rivers.

Although the first actions of Europeans to cultivate wild rice seem to have stressed its value as a food for wildlife, the potential for its cultivation as a food crop appears early in their writings. Several publications in the mid-1800s favored "agronomic production" of wild rice. They also note that the first mechanical harvesting took place on "private lands . . . in 1917."[8]

In his 1903 Bulletin, Brown describes propagation efforts made as early as 1902. By 1931, the *Scientific American* reported that "the growing demand for wild rice in recent years has resulted in experiments being made to increase the supply, and attempts at domestic cultivation on a comparatively small scale are proving successful."[9]

The problems of successful cultivation of wild rice were first made apparent in the failed 1751 effort by Peter Kalm, of the Royal Academy of Sweden, to propagate the plant in Sweden. His account states: "If we could succeed in getting this rice to grow and ripen here we would have gained a great deal, for the wettest places would become as productive as fields if the plant would stand our winters. . . . The greatest difficulty will be to find a method of sowing seeds so they will germinate. We still know very little about nature's method of sowing the seeds of plants growing in water."[10]

Kalm's efforts apparently bore no fruit, because he transported the seeds in a dry state. Finally, in 1791, a Dr. Nooth put up some seeds from Canadian lakes in jars of water, which he sent to Europe. "As soon as they arrived," reports Chambliss, "they were sown in a proper situation, where they came up in a few days and the plants ripened their seeds extremely well in the autumn," although permanent beds were not established.[11]

In addition to being kept wet in order to retain viability, wild rice seeds of *Z. palustris* must undergo a thorough cold dormancy or the seeds will not germinate. Once sprouted, they must be grown in a habitat of their preference: water that is nutrient-rich with a little flowage and of an appropriate depth, usually six inches to several feet.

These requirements, once understood, were fairly easy to accommodate, and in the 1950s, the first cultivated wild rice paddy was created near Merrifield, Minnesota. The paddy was drained in the fall, and harvested by hand the first years, and then by machine.[12] As with rice in natural stands, the crops were harvested in several passes, as the rice matured over ten to fourteen days.

The shattering, or gradual maturing, of the wild rice crop was the largest impediment to the development and growth of wild rice as an agricultural crop. In order for harvesting to be efficient, it had to be done with machinery, and the rice would need to be collected in a single pass. This was not efficient with rice that matured over a ten- to fourteen-day period.

The solution to the problem turned out not to be in chemistry or research, but in the wild rice beds themselves. As with many plants, *Z. palustris* has within its species category a number of naturally occurring varieties, or sub-species. These varieties account for variations such as wider or thinner leaves, and longer or shorter kernels. In 1963, two professors at the University of Minnesota Department of Agronomy and Plant Genetics discovered plants in a grower's field that retained their seed longer than the rest of the plants. This discovery was made on a paddy cultivated by Alcott Johnson, and the variety is named after him.[13]

The seeds were increased by growing them, selecting from the crop for non-shattering, and then repeating that cycle over and over again. This is the way corn seed was selected for hundreds of years prior to its hybridization around 1900. The genetic manipulation and hybridization of wild rice seed is probably inevitable, but for now all seed used in cultivated paddies is developed through selection, not hybridization.[14]

Even selection has its limitations, and has not been useful in solving two other problems that face wild rice growers: the need for wet storage of the seed, and for a cold dormancy period. Turning to *Z. aquatica*, which grows on the East Coast and does not require a cold dormancy, does not help. Those plants are highly shattering, and the seeds are thin and unsuitable for development as a crop. However, the problems of storage and dormancy will likely be solved through research, including the mapping of wild rice genes, which is currently underway.[15]

Although the *Z. palustris* cultivars still exhibit some shattering, the problem for the most part is under control, and in the 1970s wild rice paddy experiments burgeoned and then flourished, first in Minnesota, and then in California. Currently, each produces six to seven million pounds of finished rice annually.

The basic premise of growing paddy rice is the same in Minnesota and California, and appears to be simple: Build dikes around fields; plant the seeds; flood the fields; as the rice seeds begin to mature, gradually lower the level in the fields until they are dry; harvest using a modified grain combine.

Aside from those basic aspects, however, growers in the two locations struggle with different challenges. In Minnesota, said Rodney Skoe, Clearwater Rice, Clearbrook, Minnesota, one of the major challenges is pest control. Wild rice grown in Minnesota is vulnerable to an indigenous leaf fungus, and to rice worms. Both are treated chemically, and the wild rice crop is alternated every few years with a potato crop to break the pest cycles.[16]

Most of the time, Skoe does not have to reseed his rice paddies because, as with hand-harvesting in lakes and rivers, enough seed escapes to the ground during machine harvesting to replant the beds. New paddies are sown in the fall, so the seeds can undergo their natural dormancy during the winter.

Skoe harvests his paddies with modified grain combines: The wheels are replaced with tracks, which move more efficiently through the mucky

A Clearwater Wild Rice paddy, Clearbrook, Minnesota. Cultivated wild rice is grown in paddies that are flooded with water to simulate natural growing conditions. As the rice ripens, the paddies usually are gradually drained so they can be harvested using modified rice or grain combines. Some producers, however, can harvest undrained paddies. Photographer: Vivienne Morgan.

The availability of cultivated wild rice changed the wild rice market in four important ways: the amount of processed wild rice increased five-fold; the supply became consistently available; the processed rice became available in consistently sized kernels; and the price stabilized. Clearwater Wild Rice harvest, Clearbrook, Minnesota, August 1998. Photographer: Vivienne Morgan.

Rodney Skoe, Clearwater Wild Rice, Clearbrook, Minnesota, and the author inspect the August 1998 harvest. Skoe's parents, Stanton and Beatrice Skoe, his uncle Ray Skoe, and Don and Gladys Barron started the first large-scale cultivated wild rice company in Minnesota. Photographer: Vivienne Morgan.

soil of the paddy, and the wheat header, including the reel, is replaced with a taller one that accommodates the taller growing wild rice.

Some of the challenges for the California wild rice grower are different, said Jack DeWit, of DeWit Farms in the Sacramento Valley, which farms white and wild rice. Because wild rice is not indigenous to California, growers there do not generally have problems with pests such as brown spot and rice worms. Rather, wild rice crops are planted alternately with white rice crops, a major industry in the Sacramento Valley, in order to break the pest cycles in the white rice fields. The challenges in California come with the care and planting of the wild rice seeds.[17]

Gourmet House wild rice processing plant, Clearbrook, Minnesota, 1998. The roasters on the right are used to parch the green rice, prior to hulling. Photographer: Vivienne Morgan.

The first wild rice paddy seeds came from Minnesota paddies and, the story goes, were brought to California in a picnic cooler. The seeds must be kept wet to retain their viability, and must be subjected to a five-month cold dormancy in order to trigger germination. The paddies in California, therefore, have to be seeded anew each year with seeds that have been kept in cold, wet storage.

The development of a seed that does not require cold dormancy is a priority for wild rice plant geneticists in California. Until such seed is available, however, DeWit and other West Coast growers store their seed in coolers in large metal bins, and plant their fields in the spring. DeWit harvests his wild rice with white rice combines modified to accommodate the taller-growing wild rice.

Both Skoe and DeWit use regulated river water to flood their fields. Both struggle with blackbird invasions. The birds do not eat much seed, but when they land on the plants, ripe seeds are shaken off. It was for this reason that the American Indians in the western Great Lakes area, prior to 1900, bound seed heads together a few weeks before harvest; the bound stalks were less vulnerable to shaking. Instead of binding, Skoe and DeWit use noise techniques to discourage the birds from landing in their paddies.

Wind, hail, and rain can also damage and even destroy wild rice crops, and spring floods in both Minnesota and California can damage the paddies and bring in undesirable seed and debris. Weeds in general, however, are not much of a problem in either state.

The commercial producers of wild rice in Canada face utterly different problems, says K. Lynn Riese of Riese's Canadian Lake Wild Rice, Saskatchewan. All

Canadian wild rice is harvested from natural lakes and rivers, not from artificial paddies. While a small amount is hand-harvested, most is harvested by airboat. The airboat glides harmlessly over the wild rice plants, and the ripe rice falls off into a basket assembly attached to the front of the airboat. As the boat moves on, the rice springs back upright, immature seeds still clinging to the stalks. The most common varieties of *Z. palustris* that grow in Canada are especially high shattering and, said Riese, it is common to make up to five airboat passes over a period of seven weeks before the harvest is complete.[18]

Getting the rice into the boat, however, is the easy part, continued Riese. Much of the rice grows in remote areas, and the seed must be bagged, and transported out by airplane. In contrast, United States wild rice is carried from paddies to processors in grain trucks.

Although natural Canadian rice stands are sometimes reseeded, they are not treated with fertilizers or pesticides, and therefore the rice is usually considered to be organic, unlike most U.S. cultivated wild rice.

Most wild rice that is commercially harvested, whether by machine from paddies or by hand or with airboats from lakes and rivers, is processed in large plants. As with small processing operations and hand-processing, nothing is added to the rice, so it is still a one hundred percent pure product. And as with all wild rice, processing at large operations includes the same basic steps used by American Indians for centuries: curing (drying), parching (scalding), hulling, and winnowing.

In commercial operations, wild rice is cured in long windrows, usually on pavement, and sometimes in sheds. While traditionally rice that is curing is turned over or stirred around, at Gourmet House in Clearwater, Minnesota, it is left alone. It cures just as well as rice that is turned, and it seems to be less vulnerable to mold and mildew. During curing, the rice continues to ripen. When the rice comes in from the paddies, some is brown, some green, some black. After it has cured, it is all black or dark brown.[19]

After the rice is cured it is parched, usually in large tumblers that look like large clothes dryers with the doors removed. A worker at Gourmet House explained that they used to test the rice for doneness by breaking open a kernel: when it was crystalline white inside, it was ready. Now they used infrared ray guns to test for the optimum roasting temperature.

In California, some wild rice producers, including Indian Harvest, parboil some of their rice instead of roasting it. Parboiling is the method used to process white rice. Wild rice processed this way is also roasted a bit, returning it to the traditional wild rice appearance.[20]

After wild rice is parched, it is hulled by passing it through rollers. Initially, all rice is hulled just enough to remove the hull. Later, it may be returned to the huller for additional scarification, which removes some of the bran layer. The amount of bran removed depends on the need of the buyer of the rice. Kernels that will be used in a wild and white rice blend, for example, will be scarified enough so that the wild and white rice will cook in the same amount of time.

The hulled rice is winnowed, and is also passed through a series of cleaners that remove debris and foreign objects. It is then separated according to size and grade, and then, at Gourmet House, is stored in tote bags that hold 1,600 to 2,400 pounds. These are kept in unheated sheds because the massive amount of rice stored retains enough heat to keep the sheds above freezing even in the deepest of Minnesota winters.[21]

As with the rest of the wild rice industry, about eighty percent of the rice processed at Gourmet House goes into value-added wild rice products, such as rice blends, rice cakes, and dried soups. In fact, wholesale customers such as Uncle Ben's were an important factor in the development of the wild rice industry. They provided a consistent customer base that required large quantities of the rice, and represented a change in wild rice sales that only could have come about with the advent of cultivated wild rice. For such companies to commit to wild rice products, they had to be insured of a consistent product with consistent availability, including wild rice held in reserve for poor crop years. The cultivated wild rice growers were eventually able to meet those demands when the hand-harvested rice companies could not.

The passage from the localized, specialty crop of hand-harvested rice to the national and now international product of the cultivated paddy growers was aided in great part by the early formation of farmers' cooperatives.[22] These groups not only shared information and expertise for the growing of the rice, but worked to develop markets.

One such co-op, in the Clearbrook and Gully, Minnesota, area, was so successful that it could no longer handle the extensive marketing demands it had created.[23] The co-op was sold to Gourmet House, which is now a division of Anheuser-Busch.

Wild rice associations also contributed to the advancement of wild rice marketing.[24] Currently Minnesota, California, and Canada have wild rice councils that belong to the International Wild Rice Association (IWRA). Barb

Carstens, executive secretary for IWRA, said that the hard core work in the industry comes at the council level, especially regarding marketing and promotion. The IWRA, she said, brings the councils together, and works to promote wild rice in general.[25]

Carstens noted that while there are currently no wild rice growers operating in both California and Minnesota, there are marketers that are based in both states. One of these is Indian Harvest, in Bemidji, Minnesota, and Calusa, California, which markets in both Minnesota and California. It sells wholesale to value-added users of wild rice, and also sells retail through its mail order catalog and its Web site. Indian Harvest also processes rice in Minnesota.[26]

Wild rice has a strong presence on the World Wide Web. The search words "wild rice" will lead to addresses for many smaller companies as well as larger ones selling their products there. Some sites are operated by American Indian businesses, and many also offer local history, lore, and other information about wild rice.

As the wild rice councils and marketers continue to seek expansion of wild rice products in North America, they also seek to expand international markets. Carstens reported that wild rice is sold in France, England, Germany, and elsewhere in Europe. McDougall's Wild Rice, an organic wild rice grower in northern California, also sells in Australia.[27]

McDougall's Christine Livingston speculated about the future of wild rice. Because it is such a good food, with high nutrition and fiber content, she feels, as do other marketers, that it will continue to gain strength as a product, especially as new products appear that make it easier to use, such as instant wild rice.

Most marketers express only one major problem with consumer perceptions about wild rice: it is viewed as being an expensive food. Still, it is likely only a matter of time before the Good Berry appears on our tables with the frequency of white rice, pasta, and potatoes. In the ancient discovery stories of Wenabozhoo, *manoomin* feeds the spirit and body of the hungry *anishinaabeg*, the original people. Certainly we are often hungry today in the same ways, both in body and spirit. Perhaps we, too, will find a blessing in the mystery and majesty of *manoomin*.

❈ Side Dishes and Stuffings ❈

Side Dishes

Stuffings

Side Dishes

 ## Pecan Wild Rice Side Dish
From the kitchen of Nancy R. Kapp.

1 onion, finely chopped

1 cup pecans

1 teaspoon salt

4 tablespoons butter

4 cups cooked wild rice (page 26)

2–3 tablespoons chopped fresh parsley

Sauté onion, pecans, and salt in butter in a skillet. Stir in wild rice and cook until heated through. Sprinkle with parsley.

Serves 6 to 8.

WILD AND WHITE RICE BLENDS

To blend wild rice with white, cook separately, then blend and heat. These two rices should not be cooked together because the white rice cooks in about 15 minutes and the wild rice takes 45 to 60 minutes.

WILD AND BROWN RICE BLENDS

Substitute brown rice for some of the wild rice, and reduce amount of water. The brown rice requires less liquid. Cook as for wild rice. These rices can be prepared together because they have similar cooking times.

Minnesota Wild Rice Side Dish

From the kitchen of Sharon Fruetel.

1 cup uncooked wild rice
3 cups water
2–3 tablespoons butter
1/2 pound mushrooms, sliced
2 tablespoons minced onion
1 clove garlic, minced
3 cups chicken broth
Salt and pepper, to taste

Rinse the wild rice. Bring water to a boil and pour over wild rice. Soak for an hour, or overnight. Melt butter; add mushrooms, onion, and garlic. Cook 5 minutes at medium low heat, stirring frequently. Drain the rice. Mix rice, mushrooms, onion, garlic, and broth in a 1 1/2-quart greased casserole dish. Add salt and pepper. Bake covered at 325°F for 1 hour. Remove cover and bake 20 to 30 minutes more.

Serves 6 to 8.

Henry Wellington's Wild Rice

From the kitchen of Henry Wellington, a Restaurant, Red Wing, Minnesota.

7 cups water
1 tablespoon beef base

1 tablespoon chicken base

(Note: Beef base and chicken base are concentrated products used to make a beef or chicken broth, and are available in larger grocery stores with a good selection of gourmet items. A good homemade broth could be substituted, but the water must be reduced or omitted.)

¾ teaspoon parsley flakes

⅓ teaspoon granulated garlic (not garlic salt)

⅔ teaspoon granulated onion

⅓ teaspoon ground black pepper

2 cups uncooked wild rice

¾ cup converted white rice

5 ounces cream of mushroom soup (concentrate)

5 ounces water

Combine the first 9 ingredients in a heavy bottom pan and cover. Put pot on stove and turn burner to medium high. Bring to a vigorous boil for 8 to 10 minutes. Be sure to stir often to prevent scorching. Remove from heat, keep covered, and let sit for about 30 minutes. When water is absorbed, place rice in a flat pan, cover, and refrigerate. When cool, mix rice well with soup and final water. Cover and refrigerate. To serve: Place serving (8 ounces) in microwaveable container and cover. Microwave for 1½ to 2 minutes in a 600 to 800 watt microwave. Stir once or twice while heating.

Serves 8, or use with Henry Wellington's Chicken Jambalaya (page 87).

Herbed Wild Rice Pilaf

From the kitchen of MacDougall's California Wild Rice, Marysville, California.

Herbed Rice Ingredients
½ cup unsalted butter
2 tablespoons minced shallots
2 cloves minced garlic
1 cup uncooked wild rice
1 teaspoon fresh chopped thyme
1 teaspoon fresh chopped basil
3 cups chicken broth (preferably homemade)

Pilaf Ingredients
4 tablespoons butter
1 small Granny Smith apple, cored, peeled, and minced
1 large carrot, minced
¼ pound mushrooms, minced
¼ cup celery, minced
1 medium onion, minced
¼ cup raisins or currents
Salt and pepper, to taste

Melt butter in heavy 3-quart pan. Sauté shallots, garlic, and wild rice, stirring for about 5 minutes. Add the thyme, basil, marjoram, and chicken stock. Bring to a boil, cover, and reduce heat to a simmer. Cook from 45 to 60 minutes, or until rice is fluffy. While rice is cooking, melt butter in skillet, add apple, carrot, celery, mushrooms, and onion. Sauté, covered, stirring occasionally, until vegetables are limp, and onions turn sweet. Add raisins and rice. Stir with a fork. Season to taste with salt and pepper.

Serves 6 to 8 as an accompaniment to fish, fowl, or veal.

 ## Kat's Quinoa and Wild Rice Pilaf
From the kitchen of MacDougall's California Wild Rice, Marysville, California.

Quinoa is an ancient grain from South America. It was the food of the Incas. Wild rice was the grain of the Chippewa Indians. Combining these two grains creates a delicious and festive accompaniment to game or the vegetarian meal.

4 cups cooked wild rice (page 26) (1 cup uncooked)
2 cups cooked quinoa (1 cup uncooked)
1 large red onion, finely diced
4 cloves garlic, minced
1 bell pepper, chopped
1 small, hot, red pepper, chopped
1/2 cup diced celery
1/2 pound fresh mushrooms, sliced
1 ounce shiitake mushrooms, soaked and chopped
4 tablespoons pine nuts, toasted
4–6 tablespoons raisins
1 tart apple, chopped
2 tablespoons oil
3–5 tablespoons fresh chopped herbs, parsley, rosemary, cilantro

Preheat oven to 350°F. Toast pine nuts for 5 minutes or until lightly browned. (If rice and quinoa are uncooked, rinse, add to 6 cups boiling water, and simmer for 45 to 60 minutes.) Heat oil in a skillet. Sauté onions until nearly transparent. Add garlic, peppers, celery, and carrots; sauté 1 to 2 minutes. Add sliced, fresh shiitake mushrooms. Add fresh chopped herbs, raisins and apples. Combine all ingredients with the cooked wild rice and quinoa. Toss gently, taste for seasoning, and serve hot. This dish may be prepared up to 4 hours ahead, then reheated gently.

Serves 8 generously.

WILD RICE IN SQUASH

If serving wild rice in a squash shell, loosen the squash from around the edges, but keep it pressed back from the center; fill the center with wild rice. If serving in a bowl, press the squash around the edges of the bowl, and fill the center with wild rice.

Stuffings

Wild Rice and White Wine Stuffing
From the kitchen of Judy Pence.

½ medium onion, diced

½ clove garlic, mashed

2 stalks celery, finely diced

¼ cup butter

2 cups cooked wild rice (page 26)

½ cup dry white wine

    or ½ cup water or chicken broth

Salt and pepper to taste

Sauté onion, garlic, and celery in butter until onion is transparent. Add cooked wild rice, wine, salt, and pepper. Mix thoroughly and simmer 5 minutes. Fills the cavity of a roasting chicken or 4 to 5 small game hens.

QUICK WILD RICE STUFFING
Add ½ cup cooked wild rice to each 2 cups of your favorite bread stuffing.

Wild Rice Dressing with Bacon
From the kitchen of Indian Harvest, P.O. Box 428, Bemidji, MN 56619.

$1/2$ pound bacon slices, chopped to 1 inch
1 cup onion, chopped
1 cup celery, chopped
$1/2$ pound (8 ounces) day-old bread, cubed
$1^{1}/2$ cups cooked wild rice (page 26)
$1/2$ cup butter, melted
$1^{1}/2$ cups chicken bouillon, heated
$1/2$ teaspoon salt
$1/2$ teaspoon pepper
$1/2$ teaspoon sage

Sauté bacon until crisp. Remove pieces and drain drippings. Sauté onion and celery until tender in bacon drippings, then remove from pan. Combine bacon, bread, onion, celery, and wild rice. Toss lightly with remaining ingredients. Bake at 350°F in an uncovered pan. Use as a stuffing in pork chops, squash, or poultry.

❋ Desserts, Snacks, and Beer ❋

Desserts

Snacks

Beer

Desserts

 ## Wild Rice Maple Cake
From the kitchen of Gourmet House, Clearbrook, Minnesota.

½ cup butter

2 cups brown sugar

2 eggs

2 cups flour

1 teaspoon baking soda

½ cup walnuts

¼ teaspoon salt

1 cup buttermilk

1 teaspoon maple flavoring

2 cups cooked wild rice (page 26), well-drained

Cream butter and sugar; add eggs and beat until smooth, light, and fluffy. Mix flour, soda, walnuts, and salt together and add alternately with buttermilk to creamed mixture. Blend in maple flavoring and wild rice. Pour into 9 x 13-inch well-greased and lightly floured cake pan. Bake at 350°F for about 25 minutes, or until cake tests done. While still warm, cut into squares and serve with your favorite caramel sauce or with whipped cream.

Quick and Surprisingly Good Wild Rice Pudding
From the kitchen of the author.

This pudding is better than it looks (it is gray). You can dress up its appearance with a dollop of whipped cream, or with fresh berries.

3 cups cooked wild rice (page 26)
1½ cups milk, or soy, rice, or cashew milk
½ cup brown sugar, honey, or maple syrup
¼ teaspoon salt
1 teaspoon butter or vegetable oil
1 teaspoon ground cinnamon, nutmeg, or allspice

Put all ingredients in a large saucepan. Gently heat to a simmer. Cook about 5 minutes, stirring frequently. Serve warm or cold.

Serves 6.

Variations:

When blending ingredients, add ¼ to ½ cup presoaked dried fruit, such as raisins, apricots, or dates. For larger fruits, dice to size of raisins.

Top with cream, whipped cream, or maple syrup.

Creamy Baked Custard Wild Rice Pudding
From the kitchen of the author.

---

2 eggs or 1 egg and 2 whites
1 cup cooked wild rice (page 26)
1½ cups milk, or soy or rice milk
½ cup brown sugar or maple syrup
½ teaspoon nutmeg
¼ teaspoon salt
¾ cup raisins or other dried fruit, diced (optional)

Lightly grease a 1-quart casserole or baking dish. Put in the eggs and beat well. Add remaining ingredients and stir well. Bake in 350°F oven for 1 hour or until a knife inserted in the center comes out clean.

Serve warm or cold, plain or with cream, whipped cream, or maple syrup.

Serves 6.

Snacks

 ## Popped Wild Rice
From the kitchen of the author.

A traditional American Indian snack and trail mix.

Wild rice, uncooked
Cooking oil
Salt

Any kind of wild rice works in this recipe, including economical broken wild rice. Make it in small batches, about 1 tablespoon of kernels at a time in a 9-inch pan. ¼ cup of kernels makes about 1 cup of popped rice. Pour oil to a depth of ¹⁄₁₆ to ⅛ inch into a heavy pan or skillet, enough to cover the kernels; heat oil almost to high heat. When oil looks hot, drop in a few wild rice kernels. If they almost immediately squirm and open to four times their size, the oil is ready. If they only sizzle and sit there, the oil is not hot enough. Increase heat if necessary. When oil is ready, turn it down just a little, and sprinkle one thin layer of rice into the oil, being careful to not drop it all in one place. As soon as all the kernels are opened, lift the pan off the burner. Remove the popped rice with a slotted spoon and place on paper towel to drain. Salt to taste and serve. Note: The kernels will not pop out of the pan, so no lid is necessary. Be prepared, however, to work quickly, as the kernels burn easily in the hot oil. It is necessary to have enough oil to cover the kernels, or they burn before they pop. Do not stir the kernels, as stirring cools the oil and slows or stops the popping. It is all right to tilt the pan to distribute the oil. Replenish oil as necessary between batches.

Wild Rice Deviled Eggs

From the kitchen of Nancy Kapp.

---

8 hard-cooked eggs
½ cup cooked wild rice (page 26)
¼ cup green pimento olives, chopped
½ teaspoon salt
¼–⅓ cup mayonnaise

Slice eggs in half lengthwise. Scoop out yolks. Mash yolks. Stir in wild rice, olives, and salt. Add enough mayonnaise to moisten mixture. Stir until smooth. Fill egg whites with mixture. Chill.

Makes 16 halves.

Beer

Wild Rice Beer

From the home brewery of Jerry Bourbonnais.

I have brewed several batches of this beer and consider it a work in progress. However, I will share the version that I liked best and which has brought the highest number of compliments. This is a sophisticated recipe for advanced brewers; it will not be easily made by novices.

4.0 pounds Klages Malted Barley

3.0 pounds Wild Rice

0.2 pound Chocolate Malted Barley

0.2 pound 10 L Caramel Malted Barley

0.2 pound Vienna Malted Barley

0.5 pound Cara Pils

1.0 ounce Cascade Leaf Hops (60 min) (homegrown, AAU unknown)

0.5 ounce Hallertau Leaf Hops (5 min)

¼ teaspoon Irish Moss (30 min)

1 quart yeast #2124 yeast culture (Bohemian Lager)

Cook wild rice in 1 gallon water until gelatinous. Add to barley and 1¼ gallons 140°F water in brew pot, hold for 30 minutes. Add 1½ gallons boiling water (stabilize at 152°F), hold for 30 minutes. Raise to 158°F, hold for 30 minutes. Raise to 170°F, sparge with 4.5 gallons 170°F water.

Zizania palustris

Boil for 1 hour, add hops and Irish moss as indicated. Cool to pitching temperature and add yeast. Ferment as a lager if possible; if not, substitute Wyeast German Altbier yeast and brew as an ale (or use the yeast and method of your choice).

❈ Wild Rice for a Crowd ❈

From the Minnesota Cultivated Wild Rice Council, Minnesota Wild Rice, *The Caviar of Grains.*

Wild Rice au Gratin

2 pounds uncooked wild rice
3 pounds fresh mushrooms, sliced
Optional: substitute celery for some of the mushrooms
¾ pound butter
1½ pounds Cheddar cheese, grated

Cook the wild rice (see page 26). Sauté the mushrooms in the butter until the mushrooms soften slightly. Toss wild rice with sautéed mushrooms and cheese; spoon into buttered baking pans or 50 individual servings dishes. Cover and bake at 325°F about 20 minutes. Uncover and bake 10 minutes longer. (Baking times will be less for individual servings.)

Makes 50 side dish portions.

Wild Rice Stuffing

Use with poultry, game, roasts, or chops.

1½ pounds uncooked wild rice
1 pound bacon
1 pound medium onions, chopped

3 pounds mushrooms, sliced
1 large bunch celery, chopped
4 tablespoons crushed leaf oregano
2 tablespoons crushed leaf sage
2 pounds bread crumbs
Salt and pepper, if needed

Cook the wild rice (see page 26). Cut the bacon into 1-inch pieces and fry, adding the onion, mushrooms, and celery to sauté with the bacon. Cook until the bacon pieces are crisp and onions, mushrooms, and celery softened slightly.

Add this to the cooked wild rice, along with the oregano, sage, and bread crumbs. Adjust seasonings with salt and pepper if needed. If not using stuffing in birds, chops, or roasts, place stuffing in buttered baking pans. Cover and bake at 350°F for 40 minutes. Chicken stock—2 to 3 cups—can be added for extra moisture if needed.

Makes 50 portions.

Variations:

Sausage Stuffing: Add 1½ to 2 pounds crumbled, cooked, and drained mild-flavored sausage. Adjust seasonings accordingly.

Wild Rice Sauté

---

2 pounds uncooked wild rice
1 pound onions, chopped
1 pound fresh mushrooms, sliced
1 pound bell peppers, cut into strips (use half red and half green peppers)
1½ pounds butter
1 tablespoon salt or seasoning salt
1 tablespoon garlic salt, or to taste
Pepper, as desired

Cook the wild rice (see page 26). Sauté the onion, mushrooms, and bell peppers in the butter, adding salt, garlic salt, and pepper as desired. Cook only until vegetables are tender, but still crisp. Add the wild rice; stir and when the wild rice is heated through, serve.

Makes 50 portions.

 # Wild Rice Oriental Soup

---

1 pound uncooked wild rice
3½ gallons chicken stock, seasoned to taste
7 whole chicken breasts, deboned
156 fresh, small pea pods, or about 1¼ pounds

117 carrot curls* or ¼-inch diagonal carrot slices
¼ cup ginger juice (press fresh ginger pieces through a garlic press)

Cook the wild rice (see page 26). Poach the chicken breasts in the stock, remove chicken breasts and cool. Cut into julienne strips. Poach pea pods in chicken stock until tender, about 6 minutes; remove from stock.

Poach carrot curls in stock 1 minute (do not overcook). Remove from stock and let cool; remove picks, being careful to maintain "curls."

Clarify chicken stock, if desired. Add ginger juice to stock and adjust seasonings to taste. Reheat stock to serving temperature.

Meanwhile, arrange wild rice and chicken strips in the bottoms of 50 soups bowls. Place 6 poached pea pods in each bowl and divide hot stock between bowls, pouring slowly into the sides of the bowls. Arrange 3 carrot curls in the center of each serving and serve immediately.

Makes 50 portions for a first course soup or a light entree.

*To make carrot curls: Scrape large, thick carrots. With vegetable parer, cut wide, thin slice down the length of carrot. Roll slice around index finger and fasten with a toothpick.

 ## Lemon-Tarragon Wild Rice

2¼ pounds uncooked wild rice
¾ pound butter

5 ounces chicken base
½ cup fresh lemon juice
1–1½ cups chopped fresh tarragon
Salt and pepper to taste
Strips of lemon zest and sprigs of fresh tarragon, for garnish

---

Cook the wild rice (see page 26). Melt the butter and stir in the chicken base, lemon juice, and tarragon. Cook over low heat until ingredients are blended well, adding water for moisture only if necessary. Add the wild rice, adjust seasonings if desired, and continue cooking until wild rice is thoroughly heated. Garnish generously with strips of lemon zest and tarragon strips.

Makes 50 portions.

 ## Wild Rice Quiche Florentine

1 pound uncooked wild rice
4 medium to large leeks, finely chopped
½ pound butter
36–40 parsley sprigs, finely chopped
2½ pounds fresh spinach, finely chopped, or 2½ pounds frozen chopped
    spinach, thawed and drained well
3 tablespoons salt
2 teaspoons pepper

½ pound finely chopped walnuts
32 medium eggs
2 quarts light cream or half and half
8 9-inch pie crusts
Plain yogurt or dairy sour cream, optional topping

Cook the wild rice (see page 26). Sauté the leeks in butter about 2 minutes. Combine this with the wild rice, parsley, spinach, salt, pepper, and walnuts. Add the eggs and light cream and mix well.

Pour the mixture into the pie crusts. Bake at 425°F for 10 minutes, then reduce heat to 325°F and continue baking 30 minutes, or until a knife inserted near the center comes out clean. Let set about 15 minutes before slicing. Serve as a main dish with a dollop of yogurt or dairy sour cream.

Makes 8 quiches, or 48 portions, 6 portions per quiche.

EPILOGUE

P assion follows wild rice, in part because of its long-ago origins, which we can only fully account for through imagination, and in part because of its use as an exceptional food for the human body. The original value of wild rice was in that nutritional value. As with so many things in our world today, that value is now converted to economic value.

After the time of the community wild rice harvest, which lasted in the western Great Lakes area into the early 1900s, came the harvesting of wild rice by individuals as an economic crop. As opportunities for American Indians to support themselves were diminished as their lands were diminished, wild rice took on an additional value for them as a cash crop. From the early 1900s until the 1960s, American Indians and many non-Indians as well depended on the harvest for seasonal income. It was often used to pay taxes, or to buy winter and school clothes.

At first these harvesters sold their crops to buyers who came to the canoe landings, as they still do, with trucks and scales. The rice was weighed, and bought for cash. Later, by the 1950s, American Indian and non-Indian companies also processed and marketed the rice.

Several million pounds of finished wild rice were sold on the market those days, mostly in the western Great Lakes area, but also in gourmet food shops around North America. Because the supply was limited, and the rice labor-intensive to produce, the retail sale price was high, often $8.00 to $10.00 a pound, and sometimes more.

The advent of the cultivated wild rice paddy in the late 1960s had a devastating effect on this specialized wild rice industry. Suddenly rice could be produced en masse, with retail yields quickly reaching over a million pounds, now averaging around fourteen million pounds, of finished rice annually. The price of raw wild rice plummeted. A ricer who could have counted on making several thousand dollars during a good season could now count on only a few hundred.

The thirty years since the cultivated paddies produced their first crops have been turbulent for all involved, but in that time some things have also settled out. The American Indians have regained some of the value of their once private crop by marketing hand-harvesting and the tradition of *manoomin*. The Minnesota cultivated wild rice growers have adjusted to the entry of cultivated

California wild rice in 1977–78, which caused another upset in pricing. The overall wild rice market seems to be stabilizing.

There are, of course, still challenges to be met. Currently there are no U.S. or international standards for size and quality of wild rice, and overseas cultivated paddies may become a factor in wild rice availability and pricing. But they may also bring a grain crop to areas too cold to grow other grains. It might be seen as a fair exchange. The U.S. grows soybeans originally from Russia, and everyone grows corn indigenous to South America.

As we embrace wild rice as a food, we can also embrace its history and heritage. *Z. aquatica,* the non-food species of wild rice, still grows in many swamps and tidal areas of the eastern United States. Travelers may inquire at parks and reserves: Someone there will know where the stands are and how to view them. In the western Great Lakes area, *Z. palustris,* the food species of wild rice, can be found in most communities by asking around. It can be seen from canoes and boats and even from roadsides.

In Canada, Minnesota, and Wisconsin, the only hand-harvesting wild rice areas, only residents may purchase the license required to harvest wild rice. But non-residents may participate in hand- and machine-processing operations and in hands-on workshops at festivals and parks. Contact chambers of commerce, and search the Web with key words such as "Minnesota tourism" for locations and dates. For more formal study, the Minnesota History Center in Saint Paul has an extensive standing wild rice exhibit.

Endnotes

Notes to Chapter 1, *Manoominike-giizis:* Wild Rice Moon

1. Elden Johnson in *The Prehistoric Peoples of Minnesota*, pages 13–20, 21–23.

2. Johnson, page 20.

3. Thomas Vennum in *Wild Rice and the Ojibwe People,* page 35.

4. Theodore C. Blegen in *Minnesota: A History of the State,* page 21.

5. Blegen, page 28.

6. Vennum, pages 8–10, 35.

7. Vennum, page 9.

8. Mentioned by John Moyle in his 1942 report to the Minnesota Department of Conservation, page 10.

9. Peter Rogosin, in his 1950s *Ecological History of Wild Rice,* acknowledges a description by Marquette of wild rice stands in the Mississippi River, page 2.

10. Rogosin references Kalm's description of the wild rice plant, page 2.

11. Quoted by Gardner P. Stickney in *The American Anthropologist,* 1896, page 115.

12. Vennum, page 158.

13. Vennum, page 82.

14. Vennum, pages 89–90.

15. Moyle in his 1969 wild rice report to the Minnesota Department of Conservation, page 5.

16. Vennum, page 4.

17. Moyle, 1969, page 6.

18. Vennum, page 108.

19. Moyle, 1969, page 4.

20. Moyle, 1942, page 16.

21. Vennum, page 110.

22. Vennum, page 118.

23. Vennum, page 118.

24. Vennum, page 127.

25. Johnson, page 13.

26. Vennum, page 131.

27. Vennum, page 138.

28. Kegg, pages 123–24.

Notes to Chapter 2, The Good Berry

1. Approximate values, based on the 1996 crop; Gourmet House, Clearbrook, Minnesota.

2. Moyle, 1967.

3. Dr. E.A. Oelke, Professor of Agronomy and Plant Genetics, University of Minnesota, Twin Cities Campus, in a 1998 interview with the author.

Notes to Chapter 3, *Manoomin*

1. Earl Nyholm, Professor of Ojibway at Bemidji State University, Minnesota, in a 1998 interview with the author.

2. Upham, page 321.

3. Alfred Rogosin, in *An Ecological History of Wild Rice,* page 2.

4. E.A. Oelke, Professor of Agronomy and Plant Genetics, University of Minnesota, Twin Cities Campus, reported to the author in correspondence, 1999.

5. Vennum in *Wild Rice and the Ojibwe People,* page 13.

6. Lawrence Hoff in his master's degree thesis for Mankato State University, Minnesota, page 25.

7. Warwick and Aiken, *Systematic Botany,* 1986, page 464.

8. Oelke, Porter, Grombacher, and Addis, *Cereal Foods World,* 1997, page 236.

9. E.A. Oelke in a 1998 interview with the author.

10. Carstens, in a 1998 interview with the author.

11. E.A. Oelke et al, *Wild Rice Production in Minnesota,* University of Minnesota Agricultural Extension Bulletin 464, 1982, page 9.

12. Vennum, page 14.

13. John Moyle, in a 1969 report, states that it "commonly grows in water 6 inches to 3 feet in depth," page 1.

14. Rogosin, page 6.

15. Mike Haramis, wildlife biologist at the Patuxent Wildlife Research Center in Laurel, Maryland, in a 1998 interview with the author.

16. Paula Power, a botanist with the U.S. Fish and Wildlife Service in San Marcos, Texas, in a 1998 interview with the author.

17. Power interview.

18. Power interview.

19. Haramis interview.

20. Rogosin, page 14.

21. Rogosin, pages 18–19.

22. Rogosin, pages 17 and 13.

23. Vennum, pages 215–16.

24. Moyle, 1969, page 3.

Notes for Chapter 4, Wenabozhoo: The Origins and Discovery of Wild Rice

1. Earl Nyholm, Professor of Ojibway, Bemidji State University, Minnesota, in a 1998 interview with the author.

2. Nyholm interview, 1998.

3. Vennum, pages 61, 65, and 66.

4. Vennum, page 71.

5. Vennum, page 68.

6. Rajnovich, pages 201–4.

7. Rajnovich, page 204.

8. Seppo Hemming Valpuu, in a 1989 master's degree thesis for the University of Minnesota, page 1.

9. Rajnovich, pages 211–12.

10. Valpuu, page 58.

11. Rajnovich, page 2.

12. Valpuu, page 1.

Notes for Chapter 5, *Zizania palustris*

1. Thomas Vennum, pages 217–18.

2. Moodie, page 72.

3. Moodie, page 72.

4. Warren W. Warren, Wild Rice Manager at the White Earth Reservation in northern Minnesota, in a 1998 interview with the author.

5. Brown, page 9.

6. "An Ancient Harvest in Our Own Northwest," *Travel,* page 27.

7. Bill London, "Rice Harvesting by Airboats," *Trailer Boats,* page 70.

8. E.A. Oelke et al, "Wild Rice: New Interest in an Old Crop," page 239.

9. Pedrose, page 334.

10. Reported in Chambliss, page 371.

11. Kalm, page 371.

12. Oelke et al, "Wild Rice: New Interest in an Old Crop," page 239.

13. The professors are Paul Yagyu and Erwin Brooks, as reported in Oelke et al, "Wild Rice: New Interest in an Old Crop," page 239.

14. Oelke in a 1998 interview with the author.

15. Oelke interview.

16. Skoe, in a 1998 interview with the author.

17. DeWit, in a 1998 interview with the author.

18. Riese, in a 1998 interview with the author.

19. Julie Wraa, Gourmet House in Clearbrook, Minnesota, a wild rice processor and marketer, in a 1998 interview with the author.

20. Don Kuiken of Indian Harvest, in a 1998 interview with the author.

21. Wraa interview, 1998.

22. E.A. Oelke et al, "Wild Rice: New Interest in an Old Crop," page 240.

23. Rodney Skoe, Clearwater Wild Rice, Clearbrook, Minnesota, in a 1998 interview with the author.

24. Oelke interview.

25. Carstens, in a 1998 interview with the author.

26. Mike Holleman, Indian Harvest, Bemidji, Minnesota, in a 1998 interview with the author.

27. Christine Livingston, MacDougall Wild Rice, in a 1998 interview with the author.

Recommended Reading

Wild Rice and the Ojibway People, Thomas Vennum, Minnesota Historical Society Press, Saint Paul, 1988.

The Sacred Harvest: Ojibway Wild Rice Gathering (Juvenile Literature), Gordon Regguinti, Lerner Publications, Minneapolis, 1992.

Portage Lake: Memories of an Ojibwe Childhood, Maude Kegg, University of Minnesota Press, Minneapolis, 1991.

The Patuxent River Wild Rice Marsh, Brooke Meanley, The Maryland National Park and Planning Commission, 1996.

Selected Bibliography

Andrist, Ralph K. "Where the Wild Rice Grows." *Reader's Digest,* Vol. 59, July 1951, pp. 121–22.

Blegen, Theodore C. *Minnesota: A History of the State.* Minneapolis: University of Minnesota Press, 1975.

Brown, Edgar. *Wild Rice: Its Use and Propagation.* Washington, D.C.: Bulletin No. 50, United States Bureau of Plant Industry, 1903.

Chambliss, Charles E. *The Botany and History of Zizania Aquatica L. (Wild Rice).* Journal of the Academy, Vol. 30, No. 5, May 15, 1940.

Hoff, Lawrence. *The Domestication of Wild Rice as a Crop.* Mankato, Minnesota: Master's Degree Thesis, 1976.

Hough, Donald. "Ancient Harvest in Our Own Northwest." *Travel.* Vol. 43, June 1924, pp. 24–26.

Johnson, Elden. *The Prehistoric Peoples of Minnesota.* St. Paul: The Minnesota Historical Society, 1978.

Kegg, Maude. *Portage Lake: Memories of an Ojibwe Childhood.* Minneapolis: University of Minnesota Press, 1991.

London, Bill. "Rice Harvesting by Airboats," *Trailer Boats,* April 1986, v. 15, p. 70.

Martin, A.D. and F.M. Uhler. *Food and Game Ducks in the United States and Canada.* Research Report 30, Fish and Wildlife Service, Department of the

Interior. United States Government Printing Office, 1951. (Reprint of USDA Technical Bulletin 634, 1939.)

Moyle, John. *The 1941 Minnesota Wild Rice Crop; Fisheries Research Investigational Report No. 40, February 15, 1942.* St. Paul: Minnesota Department of Conservation, Division of Game and Fish, 1943.

———. *Wild Rice: Some Notes, Comments and Problems.* St. Paul: Minnesota Department of Conservation, Division of Game and Fish, Special Publication No. 47, 1969.

Oelke, E.A. et al. "Wild Rice: New Interest in an Old Crop." *Cereal Foods World.* April 1997, Vol. 42, No. 4, pp. 234–47.

———. *Wild Rice Production in Minnesota.* University of Minnesota, Agricultural Extension Service Bulletin 464, 1982.

Pedrose, Lawrence W. "Wanted: A Wild Rice Harvester." *Scientific American.* May 1931, pp. 334–35.

Rajnovich, Grace. "A Study of Possible Prehistoric Wild Rice Gathering on Lake of the Woods, Ontario." *North American Archeologist,* Vol. 5, No. 3, 1984, pp. 197–215.

Reed, Robert R. *Wild Rice: America's First Grain.* Winona, Minnesota: Winona Teachers College, 1943.

Rogosin, Alfred. *An Ecological History of Wild Rice.* State of Minnesota Department of Conservation, June 28, 1951. Reproduced by the Division of Game and Fish, March 3, 1954.

Scientific American. 108:365, April 19, 1913, p. 365.

Stickney, Gardner P. *The American Anthropologist.* Washington, D.C., Vol. IX, No. 4, 1896.

Upham, Warren. *Minnesota Geographic Names.* St. Paul: Minnesota Historical Society, 1969.

Valpuu, Seppo Hemming. *Paleoethnobotany of Big Rice Site, St. Louis County, Minnesota: Early Wild Rice (Zizania aquatica, L.) in Archaeological Context.* Master's degree thesis for the University of Minnesota, 1989.

Vennum, Thomas Jr. *Wild Rice and the Ojibway People.* St. Paul: Minnesota Historical Society Press, 1988.

Warwick, Suzanne and Susan Aiken. "Electrophoretic Evidence for the Recognition of Two Species in Annual Wild Rice." *Systematic Botany* (1986), 11(3); pp. 464–73.

General Index

Number in italics indicates chart, table, or illustration

Buying wild rice, 22
  blends, 22
  buyer's guide, *21, 23*
  California wild rice, *23, 24*
  Canadian wild rice, *23*
  cultivated wild rice, *23*
  flour, *24*
  grades, *24*
  hand-harvested wild rice, *23*
  instant wild rice, *24*
  labeling laws and, *24*
  labels and, *23*
  lake wild rice, *23*
  machine-harvested wild rice, *23*
  Minnesota wild rice, *23, 24*
  Oregon wild rice, *23*
  organic wild rice, *23*
  packaging standards, 151
  paddy. *See* Buying wild rice, cultivated
  quick-cooking wild rice, *24*
  river wild rice, 29
  Wisconsin, *23*
California wild rice. *See* Processing of wild rice,
  mechanical. *See* Harvesting of wild rice,
  mechanical. *See* Cultivation of wild rice,
  California cooking of. *See* Cooking wild rice,
  California
Canadian wild rice. *See* Cooking wild rice,

Canadian wild rice. *See* Harvesting of wild
  rice, Canada
Cooked wild rice
  freezing, 27
  serving, 27
  storing, 28
Cooking wild rice, 22, 24, *26*
  black wild rice, *21, 25*
  blonde wild rice, *21, 25, 27*
  broken wild rice, *25*
  brown wild rice, *21, 25*
  buyer's guide, *21*
  California cultivated wild rice, 20
  Canadian wild rice, 20
  cooking times, *25*
  cultivated wild rice, 20
  instant wild rice, *24, 25*
  instructions for, *26*
  lake wild rice, 20
  long wild rice, *21*
  Minnesota cultivated wild rice, 20
  paddy rice. *See* Cooking wild rice, cultivated
    wild rice
  parboiling, 27
  pre-soaking, 27
  quick wild rice, *25*
  river wild rice, 20
  yields, *25*

Recipe Index

W